SKETCHES AND GENEALOGY

OF

The Forney Family

FROM LANCASTER COUNTY,
PENNSYLVANIA
In Part

By

JOHN K. FORNEY
ABILENE, KANSAS

JANAWAY PUBLISHING, INC.
2013

Notice

In many older books, foxing (or discoloration) occurs and, in some instances, print lightens with wear and age. Reprinted books, such as this, often duplicate these flaws, notwithstanding efforts to reduce or eliminate them. The pages of this reprint have been digitally enhanced and, where possible, the flaws eliminated in order to provide clarity of content and a pleasant reading experience.

Originally published
Abilene, Kansas
1926

Reprinted by:

Janaway Publishing, Inc.
732 Kelsey Ct.
Santa Maria, California 93454
(805) 925-1038
www.janawaygenealogy.com

2013

ISBN: 978-1-59641-308-5

Made in the United States of America

J K Forney

SKETCHES AND GENEALOGY

of

THE FORNEY FAMILY

FROM LANCASTER COUNTY,
PENNSYLVANIA
In Part

By

JOHN K. FORNEY
ABILENE, KANSAS

FOR PRIVATE CIRCULATION

Printed for the Author
by
The Reflector Printing Co.
Abilene, Kansas
1926

PREFACE

The effort of searching for data and information, began in A. D., 1901, to get a Genealogical record of names, date of birth, marriage and deaths of the decendants of Peter Forney and wife, Ann, daughter of John Smith.

The book contains almost a complete record of the oldest son Abraham, the second son Peter only in part as traces on some of them were soon lost and of the daughters some were only traced to their marriage and no further record. Also a part genealogy of John Forney, Cacalico Township, Lancaster County and Summerset County, Pennsylvania.

The historical part is very meager as there was very little record at hand to obtain information.

ILLUSTRATIONS

INDEX OF CONTENTS

INDEX OF GENEALOGY

GENEALOGY OF THE FORNEYS IN LANCASTER COUNTY, PENNA, IN PART

1 Peter Farnie, Earlville, Pa. b. 1695; d. July 1747. Ann Smith, b. 1697; d. Jan. 1753; Dau. of John Smith.

2......Catharine Farnie, b. 1705; d.—.

3......Christian Farnie, Warwack Towp. b. 1707; d. 1757. m. Elizabeth.

4......Ann Eliza Farnie. b. 1711; d. May, 1746.

Family of PETER FARNIE (1) and ANN SMITH

5......Abraham, Earlville, Pa. b. 1720; d. 1784. m. Elizabeth Spurgeon, Dau. of Jeremiah Spurgeon.

6......Peter, Earlville, Pa. b. 1723; d. 1798 Harrisburg, Pa., m. Barbara Eby.

7......Barbara, Earlville, Pa., b. 1726, m. Christian Oblinger.

8......Anna, Earlville, Pa., b. 1730, m. Jacob Kern, Reading, Pa.

9......Mary, Earlville, Pa., b. 1741; d. 1790, m. Jacob Carpenter. b. 1741; d. 1797 Son of Gabriel Carpenter and Apolonia Hermon, or grand son of Dr. Henry Carpenter and Salome Ruffner.

10......Susan, Earlville, Pa., b. 1745; d. Oct. 5, 1822, Strausburg, Pa., m. Dr. Henry Carpenter, Earlville, Pa., b. Aug. 14; 1713; d. April 18, 1776. Third son of Dr. Henry Carpenter and Salome Ruffner.

Family of ABRAHAM FORNEY (5) and ELIZABETH SPURGEON

11......Abraham, Earlville, Pa., b. Aug. 15, 1758; d. Jan. 18, 1821, m. Anna Maria Weidman, b. Feb. 15, 1760; d. May 25, 1835.

12......John, Earlville, Pa., b. Nov. 30, 1760; d. Oct. 6, 1823; m. Elizabeth Lehman, Pequa, Pa., b. Mar. 6, 1766; d. Jan. 3, 1847. Dau. of Daniel Lehman.

13......Peter, Earlsville, Pa., b. 1762; d. June 29, 1837; m. Ann—.

14......Elizabeth, Earlville, Pa., m. Michael Quickel, Cumb. Co., Pa., now Cocolamus Twp., Juniatta Co., Pa.

15......Samuel, Earlville, Pa.

16......Maria, Earlville, Pa.

17......Salome, Earlville, Pa.

Family of ABRAHAM FORNEY (11) and ANNA MARIA WEIDMAN

18......John W., Earlville, Pa., b. Oct. 15, 1784; d. Dec. 21, 1867; m. Barbara Baker; b. Mar. 24, 1786; d. May 2, 1855. Susana, Mohn, Rothsville, Pa., b. 1838; d. Mar. 7, 1916; m. Aug. 18, 1857.

19......Catharine, Earlville, Pa., b. July 3, 1791; d. Sept. 3, 1836; m. John Forney; b. 1790. Son of John Forney (12) and Elizabeth Lehman.

20......Abraham, Scheaffustown, Pa., b. Feb. 14, 1794; d. Feb. 22, 1831; m. Lydia Levan, b. 1803; d. 1845.

Family of JOHN FORNEY (12) and ELIZABETH LEHMAN

21......John, Earlville, Pa., b. 1790; d. 1827; m. Catharine Forney. Dau. of Abraham Forney and (11) Anna Maria Weidman.

22......Levi, Lititz, Pa., b. Oct. 29, 1799; d. July 14, 1882; m. Lydia Keller, Ephrata, Pa., b. July 13, 1808; d. Aug. 24, 1824 Maria Rupp, Brownstown, Pa., b. Oct. 1, 1806; d. June 3, 1855; m. Apr. 18, 1825; Eliza Hershey; m. Dec. 8, 1859.

23......Hannah, Halifax, Pa., d. 1837; m. William Lintner; d. 1838.

Family of PETER FORNEY (13) and ANN—

24......Peter, Earlville, Pa., b. 1792: disappeared from home at the age of nineteen and was never heard from.

25......Emanuel, Anville, Pa., b. 1795; d. 1849; m. first wife Fasnicht; b—; d—; second wife Polly Rudy, Annville, Pa., b. Sept. 1, 1798; d. Aug. 4, 1875.

26......Catharine, Earlville, Pa., b. 1801; m. — Farn. A music teacher.

27......Hannah, Earlville, Pa., b. 1798; d. 1858.

28......Sallie, Earlville, Pa., b. 1805.

Family of JOHN W. FORNEY (18) and BARBARA BAKER

29......William, Earlville, Pa., b. Oct. 13, 1806; d. Sept. 14, 1831;

m. Nov. 21, 1826; Catharine Graybill; d. 1883, Lebanon, Pa.

30......Mary, Earlville, Pa., b. Nov. 19, 1807; d. Dec. 13, 1879.

31......Elizabeth, Earlville, Pa., b. Nov. 16, 1811; d. Jan. , 1868; m. Mar. 6, 1834. John Hostetter, Manheim, Pa., b. July 15, 1801; d. Sept. 23, 1866.

32......Sophia, Earlville, Pa., b. Feb. 20, 1816; d. Aug. 15, 1884; m. May 16, 1843 Benjamin M. Stauffer, Manheim, Pa., b. Dec. 25, 1818; d. Nov. 28, 1896.

33......Sarah Ann, Earlville, Pa., b. Feb. 9, 1814; d. Apr. 14, 1854; m. Mar 11, 1834 Jcob Wolf, Lancaster, Pa.

34......Henry, Leola, Pa., b. Feb. 10, 1818; d. Aug. 8, 1898; m. Oct. 1838 Elizabeth Bard; b. Nov. 13, 1818; d. Nov. 11, 1890.

35......Abraham, West Earl, Pa., b. Sept. 26, 1809; d. Jan. 23, 1894; m. Feb. 21, 1837 Mary Lane, Oregon, Pa., b. May 18, 1809; d. Sept. 27, 1890.

36......Anna, West Earl, Pa., b. Mar. 14, 1828; d. Mar. 22, 1828.

37......Lavina, West Earl, Pa., Dec. 6, 1819; d. Oct. 14, 1873; m. Sept. 1838 Henry Wise.

Family of JOHN FORNEY (21) and CATHERINE FORNEY

38......Anna, Maria, Iowa; d. 1838; m. J. S. Bartruff, Iowa; d. 1838.

Family of LAVINA FORNEY (37) and HENRY WISE

39......Lizzie, m. Samuel Ruth.

40......Barbara, m. Archabott Yundt.

Family of EMANUEL FORNEY (25) POLLY RUDY

41......Lydia R., Annville, Pa., b. June 22, 1835; d. July 11, 1911; m. Apr. 25, 1854 William Long; d. 1868; m. May 12, 1881 Jonathan Dundore; d. Jan. 8, 1889.

42......Adam R., Anniville, Pa., b. April 8, 1837; d. Sept. 12, 1914; m. Elizabeth Gingerich, b. March 12, 1847; d. Aug. 19, 1906.

Family of HANNAH FORNEY (23) and WILLIAM LINTNER

43......Hannah, Halifax, Pa., d. small children.
44......Lintner, Halifax, Pa., d. small children.

Family of LEVI FORNEY (22) and MARIA RUPP

45......Abraham, Elizabethtown, Pa., b. Jan. 23, 1827; d. Feb. 10, 1909; m. May 14, 1846 Ann Keller, b. Mar. 18, 1828; d. Sept. 12, 1901.
46......Leah, West Earl, Pa., b. July 9, 1829; d. Mar. 5, 1833.
47......John, Lititz, Pa., b. Nov. 30, 1831; d. Dec. 28, 1872.
48......Joseph, East Petersburg, Pa., b. Jan. 5, 1834; d. Feb. 19, 1908; m. Dec. 2, 1856 Susan Gochenaner; b. Aug. 2, 1836; d. Aug. 26, 1909.
49......David R., Mountjoy, Pa., b. Aug. 20, 1836; d. April 6, 1917; m. May 28, 1862 Elizabeth Bollinger; b. Jan. 19, 1841; d. Mar. 16, 1922.
50......Elizabeth, Lititz, Pa., b. Jan. 16, 1839; d. Feb. 17, 1908; m. 1858 Abraham Longenecker; b. July 17, 1834; d. Nov. 9, 1902.
51......Martin R., Lititz, Pa., b. Apr. 14, 1841; d. Jan. 12, 1925; m. Nov. 1, 1866 Sarah Ann Lane; b. Apr. 18, 1842; d. Jan. 28, 1886; m. Sept. 19, 1889 Annie M. Campbell, b. Nov. 30, 1865.
52......Aaron R., West Earl, Pa., b. Feb. 16, 1844; d. Feb. 3, 1850.
53......Maria R., Lititz, Pa., b. Oct. 3, 1846; m. Israel Graybill, Elm, Pa., b. Aug. 13, 1836; d. Apr. 6, 1911.
54......Levi R. Lititz, Pa., b. July 14, 1849; d. Nov. 8, 1913; m. Dec. 22, 1892; m. Fannie H. Wissler, b. Sept. 18, 1856; d. July 17, 1912.

Family of ABRAHAM R. FORNEY (45) and ANN KELLER

55......Salinda, Mountjoy, Pa., b. Dec. 6, 1848; m. Nov. 24, 1870, John Hertzler, b. Nov. 25, 1849.
56......John K., Abilene, Kan., b. Dec. 1, 1850; m. Oct. 2, 1873, Annie S. Hoffman, b. July 15, 1845; d. Aug. 16, 1916.
57......Martin K., Elizabeth, Pa., b. Jan. 3, 1857; m. Apr. 30, 1889 Anna Hemperly, b. May 18, 1860; d. Aug. 1918

58......Anna Mary, Elizabethtown, Pa., b. Apr. 8, 1861; d. Oct. 30, 1879, Abilene, Kansas.

59......Lizzie, Elizabethtown, Pa., b. June 9, 1865; m. 1888 Joseph Eshelman, b. Dec. 8, 1855.

Family of JOSEPH FORNEY (48) and SUSAN GOCHENANER

60......Lemon G., Lancaster, Pa., b. Sept. 19, 1857; m. May 9, 1878 Lizzie Krider.

61......Michael, Lititz, Pa., b. Jan. 26, 1859; d. Mar. 16, 1859.

62......Susan, Lancaster, Pa., b. May 9, 1860; m. Oct. 16, 1883 Tilghman M. Hostetter, b. Dec. 14, 1858.

63......Rev. Milton G., East Petersburg, Pa., b. Aug. 7, 1862; m. May 5, 1887 Ellen Swar, b. July 19, 1866.

64......Martin G., Lititz, Pa., b. Sept. 17, 1864; d. Mar. 14, 1870.

65......Maggie G., Ephrata, Pa., b. Sept. 2, 1866; d. May 4, 1919; m. Oct. 6, 1894 Hiram G. Mentzer, b. June 14, 1863.

66......Elmyra G., Manheim, Pa., b. Oct. 25, 1868; m. Mar. 24, 1892 Abraham Hostetter, b. May 10, 1864.

67......Lizzie G., East Petersburg, Pa., b. Sept. 8, 1870; m. Apr. 4, 1911 Simon Gingrich, b. Mar. 28, 1869.

68......Emma G, Lititz, Pa., b. Mar. 31, 1873; d. Aug. 12, 1873.

69......Bertha G., East Petersburg, Pa., b. Aug. 7, 1874; m. Sept. 5, 1895 Albert B. Groff, b. Mar. 6, 1873.

70......Joseph G., Lancaster, Pa., b. July 24, 1876; m. Oct. 8, 1908 Mary Ann Handly, Franklin, Ind., b. Dec. 19, 1880.

71......Levi G., Lancaster, Pa., b. June 21, 1878; m. Jan. 22, 1910 Mary Carmany, b. Apr. 9, 1884.

72......Anna G., East Petersburg, Pa., b. Apr. 1, 1882; d. Oct. 31, 1905.

Family of DAVID FORNEY (49) and ELIZABETH BOLLINGER

73......Amanda B., Junction, Pa., b. Sept. 30, 1863; d. Mar. 9, 1917; m. Oct. 7, 1880 Rubin Miller, b. May 3, 1863.

74......Monroe B., Florin, Pa., b. July 10, 1866; m. Oct. 7, 1890 Emma Stauffer, b. July 2, 1866.

75......Elizabeth B., Mountjoy, Pa., b. Dec. 15, 1869; m. Aug. 29, 1886 Samuel Shearer, b. Jan. 20, 1864.

76......Albert B., Mountjoy, Pa., b. July 25, 1871; d. Jan. 4, 1881.

77......Mary B, Elizabethtown, Pa., b. Apr. 25, 1875; m. Oct. 10 1895 Abraham Young, b. Sept. 24, 1868.

78......Anna B., Montjoy, Pa., b. Aug. 25, 1876; d. Sept. 4, 1877.

79......David B., Montjoy, Pa., b. Dec. 23, 1878; m. Lizzie Brubaker, Sept 8, 1888; d. Jan. 21, 1915; m. Dec. 18, 1915 Emma Shearer, b. Feb. 17, 1881.

80......Ella B., Mountjoy, Pa., b. Nov. 15, 1881.

Family of ELIZABETH FORNEY (50) and ABRAHAM LONGNECKER

81......Mary, Lititz, Pa., b. Nov. 4, 1859, d. Jan. 6, 1908; m. Nov. 12, 1880 Samuel Hess, b. 1857.

82......Elizabeth, Lititz, Pa., b. Apr. 16, 1861; m. Nov. 2, 1881 John K. Wissler, b. Feb. 11, 1857; d. Jan. 17, 1925.

83......Amanda, Lititz, Pa., b. June 7, 1862.

84......Christian Lititz, Pa., b. Jan. 19, 1864.

85......Fannie, Junction, Pa,, b. Jan. 4, 1867; m. Sept. 14, 1884 Milton Cassel, b. Oct. 21, 1864; d. June 11, 1925.

86......Monroe, Denver, Pa., b. Feb. 16, 1868; m. Oct. 14, 1888 Ella Bollinger, b. Aug. 2, 1868.

87......Abraham, Lititz, Pa, b. Mar. 3, 1870; d. Apr. 8, 1881.

88......John F., Lititz, Pa., b. Mar 20, 1872; m. June 24, 1902 Blanche Neal, b. July 19, 1881.

89......Levi, Lititz, Pa., b. Sept. 11, 1874; m. Dec. 25, 1898 Mamie Badorf, b. Sept. 11, 1878.

90......Amos, Akron, Pa., b. Nov. 15, 1876; m. May 12, 1898 Susan Landis, b. Aug. 12, 1879

91......Emma, Lititz, Pa., b. Dec. 28, 1878; d. Mar. 12, 1881.

92......Barbara, Manheim, Pa., b. Aug. 26, 1882; m. Oct. 11, 1903 Rev. Benjamin Stauffer, b. Nov. 8, 1881.

Family of MARTIN R FORNEY (51) and SARAH LANE and ANNA M. CAMPBELL

93......Lane L., Lititz, Pa., b. Sept. 9, 1867; m. Nov. 1, 1892 Agness M. Gibble, b. Sept. 9, 1870.

94......Theodore, Lititz, Pa., b. July 14, 1869; m. Nov. 26, 1895 Elizabeth Harnish, b. Oct. 9, 1868.

95......Mary, Lititz, Pa., b. Feb. 16, 1872; d. Feb. 12, 1902; m. Dec. 12, 1899 Clayton Sheaffer, Bareville, Pa., b. Sept. 20, 1875.

96......Emma, Lititz, Pa., Aug. 14, 1874; m. Nov. 15, 1892 Eugene Brubaker, b. Dec. 2, 1872.

97......Ella M., Lititz, Pa., b. Jan. 23, 1892; m. Mar. 13, 1913 Mahlon M. Garman, b. Mar. 5, 1893.

98......Ester M., Lititz, Pa., b. Apr. 21, 1895; d. Sept. 14, 1895.

Family of LEVI R. FORNEY (54) and FANNIE WISSLER

99......Son born dead, Dec. 25, 1894.

100......Mary, Lititz, Pa., b. Jan. 5, 1897; m. Nov. 6, 1917 Earl B. Rohrer, b. Apr. 28, 1894.

Family of ADAM FORNEY (42) and ELIZA GINGRICH

101......Annie **F. New Haven**, Conn., b—m.— Albert Kreider.

Family of LYDIA FORNEY (41) and WILLIAM LONG

102......Frank, Annville, Pa., b. Oct. 6, 1854; d. Dec. 4, 1909; m. Apr. 17, 1875; m. first w. Veronia Winter; b. July 6, 1845; d. Nov. 21, 1883; m. 1886 second w. Margret Light, b—; d. 1890; m. Sept. 14, 1891 third w. Precilla Sanders, b. Aug. 13, 1858.

Family of FRANK LONG (102) and WINTERS, LIGHT, SANDERS

103......Abner W., Annville, Pa., Oct. 9, 1876; m. Feb. 22, 1903 Anna Kirkwood, b. Aug. 31, 1885.

104......Bertha W., Annville, Pa., b. July 31, 1878; m. Oct. 4, 1896 William Englehart, b. Apr. 20, 1876.

105......William W., Annville, Pa., b. Jan. 4, 1880; d. Feb. 19, 1880.

106......Amy W., Annville, Pa., b. Jan. 14, 1882; m. Sept. 28, 1901. first h. Cyrus Moyer, b—; d. Dec. 14, 1904; m. second h. Elmer Wolf, b Nov. 27, 1873.

107......Edith Susan L., Annville, Pa., b. Mar. 16, 1888; m. Apr. 3, 1912 Pierce Carpenter, b. Sept. 13, 1888.

108......Margret Lydia L., Annville, Pa., July 24, 1889.

109......Ruth Sanders, Annville, Pa., b. June 12, 1893; m. Jan. 30, 1915 Ivan Enswinger, b. Nov. 20, 1893.

110......Charles Sanders, Annville, Pa., b. Apr. 17, 1895; d. Sept. 22, 1898.

111......Frank Sanders, Annville, Pa., b. Jan. 30, 1899.
Mrs. Precilla Sanders Long (102 third w.) b. Aug. 13, 1858; m. Jan. 22, 1912 David Enswinger, b. Jan. 15, 1858.

Family of ABNER W. LONG (103) and ANNA KIRKWOOD

112......Ardath, Annville, Pa., b. Mar. 6, 1906; d. March 27, 1906.
113......Amanda, Annville, Pa., b. Mar. 17, 1907.
114......Alene, Annville, Pa., b. Oct. 3, 1908.
115......Abner F., Annville, Pa., b. July 14, 1910.

Family of BERTHA W. LONG (104) and WILLIAM ENGLEHART

116......Cyrus, Annville, Pa., b. Jan. 10, 1898.
117......Harry, Annville, Pa., b. Sept. 10, 1899.
118......Joseph, Annville, Pa., b. Jan. 24, 1901.
119......Katharine, Annville, Pa., b. Oct. 15, 1902.
120......Son, Annville, Pa., b. Mar. 2, 1904; d. Mar. 2, 1904.
121......Guy, Annville, Pa., b. Dec. 4, 1905.
122......Myrle, Annville, Pa., b. July 17, 1907.
123......Aleine, Annville, Pa., Jan. 11, 1910.
124......Bertha, Annville, Pa., b. May 2, 1911.
125......Woodrow Wilson, Annville, Pa., b. Nov. 26, 1912.
126......Geo. Washington, Annville, Pa., b. Feb. 22, 1914.
127......Girl, Annville, Pa., b. 1915; d. 1915.

Family of AMY W. LONG (106) and CYRUS MOYER and ELMER WOLF

128......Viola M., Annville, Pa., b. Apr. 12, 1902.
129......William H. Moyer, Annville, Pa., b. Aug. 5, 1903.
130......Archa Wolf, Annville, Pa., b. Aug. 30, 1909.
131......Walter Wolf, Annville, Pa., b. Oct. 20, 1910.
132......Bertha Wolf, Annville, Pa., b. Sept. 12, 1912.
133......Charles Wolf, Annville, Pa., b. Jan. 22, 1914.

Family of EDITH SUSANA L. LONG (107) and PIERCE R. CARPENTER

134......Pierce R. Jr., Annville, Pa., b. May 12, 1913.

Family of RUTH SANDERS LONG (109) and IVAN ENSWINGER

135.....Geo. Irvin, Annville, Pa., b. Aug. 1916.

Family of WILLIAM FORNEY (29) and CATHARINE GRAYBILL

136.....Graybill, West Earl, Pa., b. July 11, 1827; d. Oct. 12, 1869; m. Oct. 12, 1855 Mary Illig, b. Oct. 6, 1836; d. Aug. 1916.

137.....Clementine, Lebanon, Pa., b. Dec. 18, 1830; d. July 6, 1911; m. Abraham Strickler, b. Oct. 16, 1827; d. Nov. 21, 1883.

Family of HENRY FORNEY (34) and ELIZABETH BARD

138.....A. Elizabeth, Leola, Pa., b. Sept. 16, 1839, d. Apr. 5, 1912

139.....Anna, Leola, Pa., age 3 mo. 6 days.

Family of ELIZABETH FORNEY (31) and JOHN HOSTETTER

140.....Benjamin, Manheim, Pa., b. Jan. 2, 1837; d. Apr. 12, 1856.

141.....John F., Manheim, Pa. b. Feb. 10, 1838; d. Sept. 17, 1867; m. Oct. 3, 1861 Fianna Keller, b. Aug. 23, 1841; d. Sept. 1, 1922.

142.....Emauel F., Manheim, Pa., b. 1839; m. Elizabeth Ensminger, d. Feb. 17, 1915.

143.....Ephriam, Chicago, Ill., b. Jan. 1841; d. June 27, 1915; m. Anna Kurtz; b.— d.— second wife Mollie Harper, Oct. 30, 1883.

144.....Maria, Lancaster, Pa., b. Apr. 30, 1843; d. Aug. 30, 1877; m. John Kurtz, b. Feb. 21, 1839.

Family of ABRAHAM B. FORNEY (35) and MARY LANE

145.....William, Earlville, Pa., b. Jan. 13, 1838; d. Sept. 1, 1847.

146.....Catharine, Earlville, Pa., b. Nov. 2, 1839; d. Nov. 30, 1839.

147.....Michael, Earlville, Pa., b. Jan. 24, 1841; d. June 26, 7842

148.....John, Earlville, Pa., b. Dec. 6, 1843; d. Nov. 21, 1860.

149......Caroline, Earlville, Pa., b. Feb. 23, 1845; d. Aug. 14, 1845.
150......Abraham, Earlville, Pa., b. July 25, 1846; d. Oct. 12, 1846.
151......Mary, Earlville, Pa., b. Aug. 16, 1849; d. Dec. 21, 1849.
152......Hariet, Earlville, Pa., b. Feb. 19, 1851; d. Mar. 15, 1851.
153......Abraham, Earlville, Pa., b. Oct. 30, 1852; d. Feb. 29, 1856.
154......Emmaline, Earlville, Pa., b. Jan. 1, 1855; d. Oct. 31, 1906; m. Oct. 17, 1873 Walter Johns, b. Feb. 24, 1850; d. Mar. 22, 1913.

Family of SARAH FORNEY (33) and JACOB WOLF

155......Catharine, Elkhart, Ind., b. Dec. 7, 1834; d. June 17, 1915; m. 1850 Jacob Whitmere, d. Mar. 1883.

156......Abraham, Elkhart, Ind., b. Dec. 21, 1835; d. Feb. 1898; m. Sallie Hildebrandt.

157......Sophia, Elkhart, Ind., b. Feb. 22, 1837; d. June 20, 1910; m. Abraham Roth.

158......Luise, born and died Mar. 10, 1838.

159......Jacob, Elkhart, Ind., b. June 22, 1839; m. Nellie Chapman.

160......Sarah Ann, Lancaster, Pa., b. Oct. 20, 1841; m. Jacob Heber Kurtz, b. Nov. 10, 1846; d. June 3, 1914.

161......John Wolf, Lancaster, Pa., b. June 10, 1843; d. Aug. 12, 1912; m. Aggie Pratt, b—.

162......William, Elkhart, Ind., b. July 10, 1846; m. — Fritzmeyer; b.

163......Anna Maria, Ephrata, Pa., b. July 13, 1848; d. Mar. 19, 1906; m. Henry K. Keller, b—.

Family of SOPHIA FORNEY (32) and BENJAMIN M. STAUFFER

164......Nathaniel, Manheim, Pa., b. Oct. 21, 1843; d. Feb. 9, 1850.

165......Edward John, Lancaster, Pa., b. Aug. 6, 1845; d. May 21, 1903; m. Clara Sophia Fondersmith, b. Jan. 29, 1844; d. Dec. 6, 1914.

166......Benjamin, Longbranch, N. Y., b. Aug. 6, 1847; d. Oct. 12, 1918.

Family of JOHN F. HOSTETTER (141) and FIANNA KELLER

169—Abert K., Lancaster, Pa., b. Feb. 3, 1864; m. Ida Kegeries, b. Aug. 27, 1866.

170—Lizzie K., Ephrata, Pa., b. Mar. 21, 1866; m. Oct. 19, 1886 Dr. John F. Mentzer, b. Mar. 18, 1862.

171—Nettie, Ephrata, Pa., b. Feb. 17, 1868; m. Dec. 22, 1881 Harry E. Hartman, b. Feb. 6, 1853.

Family of EMANUEL HOSTETTER (142) and ELIZABETH ENSMINGER

172—Nettie E, Manheim, Pa.; m. Harry S. Stauffer.

173—John, b. and d. small boy.

Family of EPHRAIM HOSTETTER (143) and ANNA KURTZ

174—Frank K., b—.

175—Daughter, b. and d. Mar. 9, 1862.

Family of MARIA HOSTETTER (144) and JOHN KURTZ

176—Edward, Lancaster, Pa., b. 1864; m. Lizzie Shirk, b.—; d.— Second wife Mollie Blanket.

177—Lizzie, d infancy.

Family of GRAYBILL FORNEY (136) and MARY ILLIG

178—Frances, Annville, Pa., b. July 2, 1857; d. Apr. 30, 1911; m. 1881 James Eshelman, b. Aug. 10, 1852; d. Oct. 24, 1906

179—Serene, Annville, Pa., b. Mar. 24, 1864; m. Aug. 10, 1886 Isaac Dobson, b. Apr. 6, 1840; d. May 2, 1915.

180—Catharine, Seattle, W., b. Dec. 24, 1869; m. Oct. 20, 1901

William Howard, b. Aug. 7, 1855.
181......Sarah, Lancaster, Pa., b. Sept. 18, 1861.
182......William, Lancaster, Pa., b. Oct. 4, 1869; d. Oct. 15, 1869.

Family of CLEMENTINA FORNEY (137) and ABRAHAM STRICKLER

183......Cyrus Forney, Lebanon, Pa., b. Apr. 18, 1854; m. Apr. 26, 1877 Annie M. Garber, b. Sept. 23, 1854.
184......William Henry, Lebanon, Pa., b. Feb. 20, 1858; d. Mar. 19, 1925; m. Oct. 25, 1883 Emma Kalbach, b. Jan. 25, 1860.
185......Laura C., Lebanon, Pa., b. Feb. 1, 1862; d. Apr. 14, 1887; m. Sept. 16, 1866 John Kellinger, b. 1860.
186......Serena C., Lebanon, Pa., b. Oct. 14, 1863; m. Feb. 19, 1888 Lewis Parker, b. Feb. 9, 1855.
187......Abraham Geary, Lebanon, Pa., b. June 18, 1866; m. June 19, 1890 Mary Lee, b. Nov. 25, 1868.
188......Catharine Mary, Lebanon, Pa., b. June 23, 1856; m. May 19, 1884, Albert Bowman Carmany, b. Feb. 18, 1861.

Family of CYRUS STRICKLER (183) and ANNIE M. BARBER

189......Marjorie, Lebanon, Pa., b. Jan. 17, 1880.
190......Guy Forney, Lebanon, Pa., b. Jan. 1, 1886; m. June 12, 1913 Helen Capron, b.—.

Family of WILLIAM H. STRICKLER (184) and EMMA KALBACK

191......Josephine, Lancaster, Pa., b. Sept. 2, 1887; m. Sept. 24, 1912 Stanton Becker von Grabill, b. Mar. 18, 1873.

Family of SERENE STRICKLER (186) and LEWIS PARKER

192......Forney Linnvill, Lebanon, Pa., b. July 18, 1889; m. Sept. 11, 1916 Mary Young Magoun, b. Mar. 27, 1894.
193......Katcharine Mitchell, Lebanon, Pa., b. Mar. 22, 1893.
194......Stewart Irving, Lebanon, Pa., b. Nov. 8, 1902.
195......Mitchell Victor, Lebanon, Pa., b. Nov. 24, 1904.

Family of ABRAHAM G. STRICKLER (187) and MARY LEE

196......Lee, Lebanon, Pa., b. June 10, 1891.
197......Roy Lebanon, Pa., b. Aug. 24, 1893.
198......Edward, Lebanon Pa., b. Sept. 21, 1902.

Family of JOSEPHINE STRICKLER (191) and STANTON BECKER VON GRABILL

199......Stanton Strickler von Grabill, Lancaster, Pa., Sept. 26, 1913.

Family of GUY FORNEY STRICKLER (190) and HELEN CAPRON

200......Helena, Lebanon, Pa., b. Dec. 4, 1914.

Family of EMMALINE FORNEY (154) and WALTER JOHNS

201......Mary Lane, Lancaster, Pa., b. Feb. 17, 1878.
202......Walter Scott, Lancaster, Pa., b. Dec. 27, 1879; m. Ellen B. Mercer.
203......Virginia, Lancaster, Pa., b. May 13, 1883; m. July 16, 1907 John F. Nissley, b. Dec. 26, 1880.
204......Charles F., New Holland, b. Sept. 30, 1875; d. Jan. 16, 1880.
205......Margret, New Holland, b. Feb. 8, 1888; d. Mar. 10, 1896.
206......Miriam, New Holland, b. Aug. 9, 1891; d. May 14, 1892.

Family of VIRGINIA JOHNS (203) and JOHN F. NISSLEY

207......Virginia Johns, Lancaster, Pa., b. Jan. 16, 1912.
208......Mary Dell, Lancaster, Pa., b. May 1, 1916.

Family of CATHARINE FORNEY (180) and WILLIAM HOWARD

209......William Jr., Seattle, W., b. Oct. 24, 1902.
210......Catharine F., Seattle, W., b. Feb. 20, 1905.

Family of SERENE FORNEY (179) and ISAAC DOBSON

211......James Forney, Annville, Pa., b. Oct. 29, 1887.

Family of MARY F. LONGNECKER (81) and SAMUEL HESS

212......Maggie, Lititz, Pa., b. May 11, 1881; d. June 6, 1881.
213......Abram L., Lititz, Pa., b. July 29, 1882; m. Fanny Keener, b.—.
214......Walter L., Lititz, Pa., b. July 27, 1884; m. Minnie Horst.
215......Ella May, Lititz, Pa., b. Oct. 12, 1885; m. Henry M. Anding, Lorein, Lou.
216......Jacob L., Springfield, O., b. June 13, 1887; m. Mabel Miller.
217......Harry L., Lititz, Pa., b. Dec. 18, 1888; m. Minnie Stoner.
218......David James, Westerville, O., b. Nov. 14, 1890.
219......Christian L., Lititz, Pa., b. Oct. 22, 1892.
220......William L., Lititz, Pa., b. Sept. 29; 1894; m. Christina Drace.
221......Amanda L., Newbern, Ala., b. Mar. 23, 1897; m. Luther Horn.
222......Anna L., Bloomington, Ill., b. Mar. 27, 1899; m. Herman Dill.
223......Elizabeth, Lititz, Pa., b. July 19, 1901.

Family of ELIZABETH LONGENECKER (82) and JOHN K. WISSLER

224......William L., Lititz, Pa., b. July 22, 1883; m. Ida Hess.
225......Edwin, Lititz, Pa., b. Apr. 18, 1895.

Family of WILLIAM WISSLER (224) and IDA HESS

226......William Howard, Lititz, Pa., b. Dec. 12, 1912.
227......Clyde Henry, Lititz, Pa., b. May 16, 1915.

Family of MONROE F. LONGENECKER (86) and ELLA BOLLINGER

228......Emma, Denver, Pa., b. Mar. 3, 1889; m. Mar. 31, 1910 Rufus Royer, b. May 20, 1884.

Family of EMMA LONGENECKER (228) and RUFUS ROYER

229......Ellen Ruth, Denver, Pa., b. Oct. 18, 1911.
230......Rufus Galen, Danver, Pa., b. Apr. 2, 1916; d. Apr. 8, 1916.

Family of LEVI LONGENECKER (89) and MINNIE BADARF

231......Mabel, Lititz, Pa., b. Oct. 16, 1901; d. Oct. 19, 1901.
232......Abraham, Lititz, Pa., b. Nov. 28, 1902; d. Dec. 1, 1902.
213......Ruth, Lititz, Pa., b. Sept. 22, 1908; d. Sept. 26, 1908.

Family of FANNIE LONGENECKER (85) and MILTON CASSELL

234—Horace, Fairland, Pa., b. Feb. 7, 1885; m. Florence Stroh, b. 1886; d. Mar. 4, 1920; m, June 29, 1922 Susie Amanda Stroh, b. Aug. 24, 1883.
235......Clarence, Fairland, Pa., b. Feb. 1, 1887; m. Mabel Sharp.
236......Robert, Sinking Spring, Pa., b. Jan. 18, 1889; m. May Winger.
237......Henry, Fairland, Pa., b. Feb. 3, 1891; d. Feb. 11, 1893.
238......Nora, Fairland, Pa., b. Apr. 14, 1893; m. Phares Winger.
239......Milton, Fairland, Pa., b. June 2, 1895; m. Nettie Hummer.
240......Florence, Fairland, Pa., b. Oct. 18, 1897; m. Mar. 16, 1916 Daniel Breitgan, b. Aug. 7, 1895.
241......Mabel, Elizabethtown, Pa., b. Feb. 18, 1899; m. Sept. 29, 1922 Jacob R. Mumma.
242......John, Reading, Pa., b. Jan. 5, 1900.
243......Edna, Junction, Pa., b. Dec. 19, 1902.
244......Elmer, Junction, Pa., b. Oct. 16, 1906.
245......Abraham, Junction, Pa., b. Mar. 8, 1908.
246......Francis, Junction, Pa., b. Apr. 19, 1909.

Family of JOHN F. LONGENECKER (88) and BLANCHE NEAL

247......Clarence Eugene, Lititz, Pa., b. Apr. 1, 1904.
248......Edna May, Lititz, Pa., b. May 1, 1907.
249......Charles Robert, Lititz, Pa., b. July 2, 1908.
250......Dorothy Lititz, Pa., b. June 8, 1912.

251......Margret Romane, Lititz, Pa., b. Oct. 1, 1917.
252......John Paul, Lititz, Pa., b. Feb. 25, 1919.
253......Sylbia Bernice, Lititz, Pa., b. Sept. 14, 1920.

Family of BARBARA LONGENECKER (92) and REV. BENJAMIN STAUFFER

254......Amon, Manheim, Pa., b. Aug. 17, 1904; m. June 30, 1925 Elsie A. Groff.
Maud Sheaffer
255......Benjamin, Manheim, Pa., b. Sept. 23, 1906. m Feb. 11. 1026
256......Naoma, Manheim, Pa., b. Aug. 25, 1909.
257......Dortha Elizabeth, Manheim, Pa., b. Oct. 25, 1919.

Family of AMOS LONGENECKER (90) and SUSAN LANDIS

258......Nettie, Akron, Pa., b. Sept. 29, 1898.

Family of SALINDA FORNEY (55) and JOHN HERTZLER

259......Annie, Mountjoy, Pa., b. Aug. 19, 1871; m. Jan. 19, 1893 John K. Young, b. June 10, 1870.
260......Lizzie, Mountjoy, Pa., b. Aug. 10, 1873; m. Nov. 24, 1892 Ezra Zercher, b. Jan. 19, 1870.

Family of MARTIN FORNEY (57) and ANNA HEMPERLY

261......Robert, Elizabethtown, Pa., b. Mar. 18, 1891; m. Oct. 11, 1915 Gorgian Henry, b. Apr. 9, 1895.
262......Abraham, Elizabethtown, Pa., b. July 17, 1898; m. June 28, 1924 Hulda Holsinger.

Family of JOHN K. FORNEY (56) ANNIE HOFFMAN

263......Elmer, Abilene, Kan., b. Nov. 19, 1875; m. Nov. 20, 1898. Hannah Lois Nutt, b. Feb. 28, 1878.
264......Christian, Abilene, Kan., b. Apr. 21, 1878; d. Sept. 14, 1912.
265......Annie, Abilene, Kan., b. Dec. 5, 1879; d. Aug. 28, 1880.
266......Minnie, Abilene, Kan., b. Aug. 19, 1881; d. July 11, 1883.
267......Mary, Abilene, Kan., b. Feb. 23, 1885; m. Oct. 17, 1916 Robert J. Long, b. Mar. 12, 1880.

268.....Abram, San Francisco, Calif., b. Oct. 12, 1888; m. Oct. 12, 1920, Meron Palmantier.

Family of ELIZABETH FORNEY (59) and JOSEPH ESHELMAN

269.....Forney, Elizabethtown, Pa., b. May 2, 1889.
270.....Walter, Elizabethtown, Pa., b. Oct. 14, 1891; d. Oct. 2, 1918.
271.....Anna Ruth, Elizabethtown, Pa., b. Dec. 19, 1898.

Family of LEMON FORNEY (60) and LIZZIE KREIDER

272.....Minnie, Lititz, Pa., b. Feb. 23, 1879; m. Nov. 27, 1902 Harry J. Asbenshade; b. Mar. 13, 1879, Lancaster, Pa.
273.....Viola, Lititz, Pa., b. Feb. 12, 1881; d. Jan. 9, 1925; m. Sept. 2, 1922 Elmer H. Hartzler, b. Mar. 25, 1885, Pittsburg, Pa.
274.....John K., Neffsville, Pa., b. Mar. 20, 1882; m. Clara Y. Baker, b. Mar. 4, 1885; d. Sept. 29, 1920; m. Mamie Wagaman, Aug. 12, 1922, b. —.
275.....Milton, Lancaster, Pa., b. Dec. 16, 1885.
276.....Lydia, b. July 2, 1888; m. Joseph A. Rudy, Nov. 13, 1908, b. June 25, 1890, Harrisburg, Pa.
277.....Annie, b. Feb. 2, 1891; m. Stauffer Heistand, b. —. Limerock, Pa.
278.....Alvin, b. May 17, 1894; m. Elizabeth Shriner, June 9, 1915, b. Dec. 23, 1896.
279.....Elmer, Lancaster, Pa., b. Apr. 17, 1897.
280.....Mary, Lancaster, Pa., b. Mar. 23, 1900.
281.....Ellen, Lancaster, Pa., b. Mar. 31, 1903.

Family of SUSAN FORNEY (62) and TILGHMAN N. HOSTETTER

282.....Nettie, Lancaster, Pa., b. June 4, 1884; d. May 20, 1920.
283.....Walter, Los Angeles, Calif., b. May 4, 1886.
284.....Jonas, Florin, Pa., b. Nov. 25, 1887; d. Feb. 2, 1889.
285.....Ruth, b. July 17, 1889; m. Edwin A. Staman, Oct. 16, 1912, Shreveport, La.
286.....Emma, b. Mar. 14, 1891; m. H. Hilton Longberry. Apr.

3, 1920, b. June 16, 1896, Lancaster, Pa.
287......Jay Forney, Phil. Pa., b. Oct. 15, 1893; m. Margret Besle, Sept. 5, 1922, England, Europe.
288......Miriam, Lancaster, Pa., b. Oct. 25, 1895.
289......George, Lancaster, Pa., b. June 21, 1898.

Family of REV. MILTON G. FORNEY (63) and ELLA SWARR

290......May, b. Oct. 2, 1888; d. Jan. 2, 1919; m. Homer Minich, East Petersburg, Pa., Jan. 2, 1910; b. Dec. 6, 1879.
291......Charles, East Petersburg, Pa., b. Feb. 12, 1890; m. Gertrude Binkley, Feb. 27, 1915, b. Sept. 30, 1893.
292......Pharas, East Petersburg, Pa., b. Sept. 17, 1894; m. Naomi H. Graybill Jan. 1, 1916, b. Sept. 13, 1893.
293......Roy, East Petersburg, Pa., b. July 12, 1897; m. Laura S. Shriner, Nov. 8, 1917, b. 1896; d. Jan. 26, 1919; m. Elizabeth Allwein, Mar. 21, 1924, b. Nov. 9, 1903.
294......Miriam Amanda, b. July 6, 1899; d. Nov. 19. 1912.
295......Paul, East Petersburg, Pa., b. Dec. 4, 1906.

Family of MAGGIE FORNEY (65) and HIRAM MENTZER

296......Edna, Ephrata, Pa., b. July 10, 1895.
297......Herbert, Ephrata, Pa., b. Dec. 16, 1899.

Family of ELMYRA G. FORNEY (66) and ABRAHAM L. HOSTETTER

298......Esther Ruth, Manheim, Pa., b. Feb. 1, 1895.
299......Henry Paul, Manheim, Pa., b. Nov. 27, 1900; m. Nettie Ginder, Nov. 27, 1924.
300......Albert Joseph, Manheim, Pa., b. Nov. 19, 1904.

Family of BERTHA FORNEY (68) and ALBERT B. GROFF

301......Nelson, East Petersburg, Pa., b. Jan. 22, 1897.
302......Elizabeth, East Petersburg, Pa., b. Dec. 14, 1900.

Family of JOSEPH G. FORNEY (70) and MARY ANN HANDLEY

303......Mary Elizabeth, Lancaster, Pa., b. Aug. 16, 1909.
304......Helen Frances, Lancaster, Pa., b. June 12, 1912.

Family of LEVI FORNEY (71) and MARY O. CARMANY

305......Jacob, Lancaster, Pa., b. Sept. 20, 1912.
306......Richard, Lancaster, Pa., b. Aug. 3, 1914.
307......Levi C., Lancaster, Pa., b. July 17, 1918.

Family of LANE FORNEY (93) and AGNESS M. GIBBLE

308......Mabel, Lititz, Pa., b. Aug. 27, 1893; M. Elmer K. Bollinger June 2, 1923, b. Oct. 21, 1898.
309......Nora, Lititz, Pa., b. Apr. 22, 1895.
310......Norman, Lititz, Pa., b. Aug. 8, 1899.
311......Maria, Lititz, Pa., b. Aug. 8, 1901; m. Frank H. Kline, Oct. 12, 1922.
312......Emma, Lititz, Pa., b. Aug. 4, 1903; m. Edward G. Bollinger, Jan. 1, 1924, b. July 26, 1900.
313......Benjamin, Lititz, Pa., b. Nov. 26, 1905.
314......Esther, Lititz, Pa., b. Jan. 4, 1907.
315......Lincoln, Litz, Pa., b. Feb. 23, 1911.
317......Galan, Lititz, Pa., b. Aug. 4, 1913.
318......Verna, Lititz, Pa., b. Jan. 25, 1915, d. Feb. 22, 1915.

Family of THEODORE FORNEY (94) and ELIZABETH HARNISH

319......Raymond, Lititz, Pa., b. Nov. 14, 1902.

Family of MARY L. FORNEY (95) and CLAYTON SHEAFFER

320......Mary, Bareville, Pa., b. Feb. 2, 1902.

Family of ELLA MAY FORNEY (97) and MAHLEN GARMAN

321......Dorothy Arline, Lititz, Pa., b. Feb. 28, 1914.
322......Martin William, Lititz, Pa., b. Dec. 24, 1915.
323......J. Wilber Lavern, Lititz, Pa., b. Dec. 6, 1916.
324......Janet Pauline, Lititz, Pa., b. June 16, 1920.
325......Richard Claïre, Lititz, Pa., b. Sept. 13, 1922.

Family of ALBERT K. HOSTETTER (169) and IDA KEGERRIES

326......Harry B., Lancaster, Pa., b. Feb. 16, 1893.

Family of LIZZIE HOSTETTER (170) and DR. JOHN MENTZER

327......Ivan, Ephrata, Pa., b. Dec. 1, 1892; m. Laura Burkholder, Feb. 17, 1916.

Family of NETTIE HOSTETTER (171) and HARRY E. HARTMAN

328......Irene, Bareville, b. Apr. 20, 1897.

Family of ANNIE F. HERTZLER (259) and JOHN K. YOUNG

329......Naomi, Junction, Pa., b. Nov. 15, 1896; m. Oscar Ruhl, Nov. 4, 1913, b. July 22, 1892.
330......Roy H., Maytown, Pa., b. Nov. 15, 1896; m. Lilian Horner, Mar. 1, 1919.
331......John H., Mountjoy, Pa., b. Jan. 4, 1899; m. Mabel Zerphy Feb. 20, 1920.
332......Mabel, Mountjoy, Pa., b. June 20, 1901; d. July 17, 1925.
333......Anna, Mountjoy, Pa., b. July 28, 1908.

Family of LIZZIE F. HERTZLER (260) and EZRA ZERCHER

334......Howard, Mountjoy, Pa., b. Apr. 3, 1894; d. Aug. 9, 1898.
335......Annie, Mountjoy, Pa., b. Aug. 11; d. Aug. 24, 1901.

336.....Beulah, Mountjoy, Pa., b. Mar. 13, 1900.
337.....Martha, Mountjoy, Pa., b. Jan. 29, 1905.

Family of NAOMI YOUNG (329) and OSCAR RUHL

338.....Chester Y., Junction, Pa., b. Mar. 28, 1914.
339.....Verna, Junction, Pa., b. Oct. 17, 1917.

Family of ROY H. YOUNG (330) and LILIAN HORNER

340.....Arline, Maytown, Pa., b. Feb. 1921.

Family of JOHN YOUNG (331) and MABEL ZERPHY

341.....Ruth, Mountjoy, Pa., b. Apr. 1919.

Family of MAY S. FORNEY (290) and HOMER MINICH

342.....Beulah, East Petersburg, Pa., b. Aug. 16, 1910.
343.....Ruth, East Petersburg, Pa., b. Feb. 23, 1912.
344.....Mary, East Petersburg, b. Feb. 11, 1913.
345.....Naomi, East Petersburg, Pa., b. Jan. 20, 1914.
346.....Hiram, East Petersburg, Pa., b. Mar. 26, 1915.
347.....Earl, East Petersburg, b. Sept. 24, 1917.

Family of CHARLES FORNEY (291) and GERTRUDE BINKLEY

348.....Harry Milton, East Petersburg, Pa., b. Dec. 1, 1915.
349.....Ellen Elizabeth, East Petersburg, b. Dec. 7, 1919.
350.....Charley Jr., East Petersburg, Pa., b. Apr. 17, 1923.

Family of REV. PHARES FORNEY (292) and NAOMI GRAYBILL

351.....Isaac Roy, East Petersburg, Pa., b. Sept. 25, 1916.
352.....Mildred Irene, East Petersburg, Pa., b. May 8, 1919.
353.....Ella May, East Petersburg, Pa., b. Mar. 5, 1921.
354.....Anna Mary, East Petersburg, Pa., b. Nov. 25, 1922.
355.....John Graybill, East Petersburg, Pa., b. Jan. 1, 1925.

Family of REV. ROY FORNEY (293) and LAURA S. SHRINER

356......Anna Ruth S., East Petersburg, Pa., b. Jan. 26, 1916; Second wife, Elizabeth Allwein.
357......Meriam Frances A., East Petersburg, Pa., b. Jan. 13, 1925.

Family of ELMER H. FORNEY (263) and LOIS NUTT

358......Frances Leone, Abilene, Kansas, b. Nov. 21, 1899; m. Harland Carter Little, Feb. 15, 1923, Kansas City, Mo.
359......Ann Louise, Abilene, Kansas, b. Dec. 9, 1902.
360......Mary Olive, Abilene, Kansas, b. May 14, 1912.

Family of RUTH HOSTETTER (285) and EDWARD A. STAMAN

361......Jeanette, Shreveport, La., b. Aug. 9, 1913.
362......Caraline, Shreveport, La., b. Oct. 6, 1917.
363......Ruth Hostetter, Shreveport, La., b. July 31, 1921.

Family of AMANDA B. FORNEY (73) and RUBIN MILLER

364......Bara, Manheim, Pa., b. Mar. 1, 1882; m. Harvey Weidle, Apr. 1918.
365......Harvey, Junction, Pa., b. Sept. 5, 1884; m. Emma Hollinger, May 15, 1909, b. June 2, 1891.
366......Allen, Junction, Pa., b. July 17, 1886; d. Nov. 6, 1888.
367......Mabel, Junction, Pa., b. Sept. 5, 1888.
368......Nora, Junction, Pa., b. June 6, 1895; m. Samuel Baker Feb. 1, 1920, b. Jan. 4, 1899.

Family of HARVEY MILLER (365) and EMMA BOLLINGER

370......Gertrude, Junction, Pa., b. Dec. 8, 1910.
371......Charles, Junction, Pa., b. Sept. 15, 1913.
372......Murriam, Junction, Pa., b. 1918.

Family of MONROE B. FORNEY (74) and EMMA STAUFFER

373......Ruth S., Florin, Pa., b. Sept. 6, 1892; m. John Eshelman 1914.
374......Martha, Florin, Pa., b. Sept. 22, 1898; d. Oct. 5, 1898.
375......Stauffer, Florin, Pa., b. Dec. 31, 1899; d. Dec. 31, 1899.
376......Edith, Florin, Pa., b. Dec. 6, 1900.
377......Roy S., Florin, b. Aug. 26, 1905; m. Maria Young, Nov. 27, 1924.
378......Lois S., Florin, Pa., b. Aug. 21, 1910.

Family of RUTH FORNEY (373) and JOHN ESHELMAN

379—Mildred, Florin, Pa., b. May 12, 1916.
380......Robert, Florin, Pa., b. July 22, 1918.
381......Orpha, Florin, Pa., b. Aug. 22, 1920.

Family of ELIZABETH B. FORNEY (75) and SAMUEL SHEARER

382......Stella, Elizabethtown, Pa., b. Mar. 9, 1887; m. Jacob L. Horst, Oct. 10, 1907, b. Feb. 1885.
383......Simon, b Dec. 9, 1888; m. Bertha Brecker, b. 1891.
384......Anna F., Florin, Pa., Mar. 6, 1891.
385......Elizabeth, Donegal Springs, Pa., b. June 11, 1894; m. Witmer Sollenberger, b. Mar. 21, 1892.
386......Elam, Florin, Pa., b. Feb. 27, 1896.

Family of MARY B. FORNEY (77) and ABRAHAM YOUNG

387......Grace, Mountjoy, Pa., b.—; m. Claude Grosh, b. Oct. 11, 1895.
388......Ester F., Elizabethtown, Pa., b. Sept. 22, 1900; m. G. D. Miller, Nov. 7, 1920.

Family of DAVID B. FORNEY (79) and LIZZIE BRUBAKER

389......Bulah, Florin, Pa., b. Aug. 14, 1909; d. —; second wife Emma Shearer.

Family of ELIZABETH SHEARER (385) and WITMER SOLLENBERGER

390......Ruth Arline, Donegal Springs, Pa., b. 31, 1920.

Family of GRACE YOUNG (387) and CLAUDE GROSH

391......Helen, Mountjoy, Ia., b. —, 1920.

Family of VIOLA FORNEY (273) and ELMER H. HERTZLER

392......Sarah Kathryn, Pittsburg, Pa., b. Nov. 22, 1912.
393......Elmer Robert, Pittsburg, Pa., b. Dec. 12, 1913; d. Dec. 19, 1913.
394......Richard Forney, Pittsburg, Pa., b. May 6, 1915.
395......Ruth, Pittsburg, Pa., b. Sept., 1920.

Family of JOHN K. FORNEY (274) and CLARA Y. BAKER

396......Joe B., Neffsville, Pa., b. Feb. 10, 1905.
397......B. Newton, Neffsville, Pa., b. Mar. 3, 1907
398......Elizabeth B., Neffsville, Pa., b. Apr. 23, 1909.
399......Mabel B., Neffsville, b. Oct. 25, 1912.
400......Clara Ruth, Neffsville, Pa., b. Feb. 22, 1915; d. Mar. 18, 1915.

Family of LYDIA FORNEY (276) and JOSEPH RUDY

401......Joseph Abraham, Harrisburg, Pa., b. Mar. 23, 1910.
402......John Forney, Harrisburg, Pa., b. Oct. 9, 1914.

Family of ANNIE FORNEY (277) and STAUFFER HEISTAND

403......John, Lime Rock, Pa., b. Feb. 1919.
404......Annie, Lime Rock, Pa., b. Sept. 1920.

Family of ALVIN FORNEY (278) and ELIZABETH SHEARER

405......Alvin Jr., Neffsville, Pa., b. 1916.

Family of EDWARD JOHN STAUFFER (165) and CLARA SOPHIA FONDERSMITH

406.....Charles, Lancaster, Pa., b. Oct. 8, 1869; m. Gertrude Martha Frantz, Oct. 12, 1910; b. Dec. 28, 1883.
407.....Benjamin, Lancaster, Pa., b. Aug. 18, 1877; m. Rosa Alma Sener, Oct. 31, 1900, b. Aug. 19, 1879.

Family of CHARLES F. STAUFFER (406) and GERTRUDE MARTHA FRANTZ

408.....Charles Frantz, Lancaster, Pa., b. Aug. 11, 1911.
409.....Sarah Ann, Lancaster, Pa., b. June 13, 1915.

Family of BENJAMIN GRANT STAUFFER (407) and ROSA ANNA SENER

410.....Elizabeth Sener, Lancaster, Pa., b. Feb. 2, 1903; m. Bruce Allen Ludgate, Pittsburg, Pa. June 12, 1926

Family of SARAH ANN WOLF (160) and JACOB HEBER KURTZ

411.....Clarande, Lancaster, Pa., b. Jan. 24, 1871; d.—.
412.....William H., Lancaster, Pa., b. Sept. 15, 1872; m. Laura Graybill.
413.....Nora, Lancaster, Pa., b. June 3, 1874; m. Dr. H. R. Bryson, Jan. 1, 1924.
414.....Ida May, Lancaster, Pa., b. Dec. 10, 1876.

Family of CATHARINE WOLF (155) and JACOB WHITMAN

415.....Elias, Goshen, Ind., b. Mar. 10, 1853; d. Feb. 19, 1874.
416.....Maria, Goshen, Ind., b. 1855; d. Dec. 25, 1915; m. William C. Hays, 1881.
417.....Ada E., Goshen, Ind., b. Mar. 3, 1857; m. Elias J. Shrock 1880.
418.....Catharine, Goshen, Ind., b. Apr. 24, 1858; m. William F. Wagner, 1879.
419.....Jacob, Goshen, Ind., b. May 5, 1860; m. Daisy Powell.
420.....John L., Goshen, Ind., b. 1863; d. 1897.

421......Dora, Goshen, Ind., b. 1866; d. 1871.
422......Cyrus, Goshen, Ind., b. 1868; d. 1871.
423......Harvey, Goshen, Ind., b. 1873; d. 1874.

Family of MARY W. FORNEY (100) and EARL B. ROHRER

424......Levi, Lititz, Pa., b. July 17, 1918.
425......Edith, Lititz, Pa., b. Oct. 3, 1920.
426......Vera, Lititz, Pa., b. Mar. 26, 1923.
427......Earl, Lititz, Pa., Apr. 22, 1924; d. Sept. 4, 1924.

Family of EMMA HOSTETTER (286) and H. HILTON LONGBERRY

428......James Tilghman, Philadelphia, Pa., b. Dec. 4, 1922.

Family of HORACE CASSELL (234) and FLORENCE STROH

429......Theodore, Junction, Pa., b. Oct. 27, 1907.
430......Eva May, Junction, Pa., b. Oct. 31, 1910.
431......Clyde Lamont, Junction, Pa., b. May 18, 1918.

Family of CLARENCE CASSELL (235) and MABEL SHARP

432......Helen, Junction, Pa., b. 1912.
433......Mabel, Junction, Pa., b. 1914.

Family of ROBERT CASSELL (236) and MARY WINGER

434......Flora, Fairland, Pa., b. Oct. 25, 1911.
435......Dortha, Fairland, Pa., b. Feb. 3, 1913.
436......Loberta, Fairland, Pa., b. Oct. 13, 1914.
437......Margee, Fairland, Pa., b. Aug. 5, 1917.
438......Anna Mary, Fairland, Pa., b. Sept. 19, 1920.

Family of NORA CASSELL (238) and PHARES WINGER

439......Elnora, Manheim, Pa., b. Sept. 27, 1915.
440......Pauline, Manheim, Pa., b. April 7, 1917.

441.....Ruth, Manheim, Pa., b. April 6, 1919.
442.....Elizabeth, Manheim, Pa., Aug. 16, 1922.

Family of MILTON CASSELL (239) and NETTIE HUMMER

443.....Myrtle Irene, Manheim, Pa., b. April 8, 1920.
444.....Forney H., Manheim, Pa., b. July 11, 1922.

Family of FLORENCE CASSELL (240) and DANIEL BRITEGAN

445.....Ruth Elizabeth, Manheim, Pa., b. 1917.
446.....Anna May, Manheim, Pa., b. 1919.

Family of FRANCES LEONE FORNEY (358) and HARLAND CARTER LITTLE

446½.....Martha Louise, Kansas City, Mo., b. May 23, 1925.

Family of MABEL FORNEY (308) and ELMER K. BOLLINGER

446¾.....Jean, b. Feb. 24, 1925.

Family of PETER FORNEY (6) and BARBARA EBY

447.....Christian, Earlville, Pa., b.—
448.....Jacob, Earlville, Pa., b. 1748; d. 1806; m. Susan Carpenter, d. 1828.
449.....John, Earlville, Pa., b. 1751.
450.....Peter, Earlville, Pa., b. July 15, 1753; d. May 2, 1779.
451.....David, Earlville, Pa., d. 1805.
452.....Barbara, Earlville, Pa., m. Jacob Fetter.
453.....Susana, Earlville, Pa., m. John Bare.
454.....Anna Catharine, Earlville, Pa., m. Samuel Bare.
455.....Rebecca, Harrisburg, Pa., m. Philip Horning.
455½.....Elizabeth, Harrisburg, Pa.

Family of JACOB FORNEY (448) and SUSAN CARPENTER

456.....Peter, Lancaster, Pa., b. Jan. 7, 1789; d. Sept. 30, 1825;

m. Aug. 24, 1813 Margaret Wien, b. Dec. 3, 1792; d. Sept. 14, 1869.

457.....Barbara, Lancaster, Pa., b. Jan. 3, 1791; d. Sept. 11, 1862.

458.....Susanne, Lancaster, Pa., b. Mar. 14, 1792; d. Feb. 2, 1793.

459.....Jacob, Lancaster, Pa., b. Apr. 7, 1794; d. Jan. 24, 1847; m. 1815 Christina Wien, b. July 25, 1794; d. Feb. 22, 1868.

460.....Sarah, Lancaster, Pa., b. Nov. 21, 1796; d. Jan. 31, 1862.

461.....Catharine, Lancaster, Pa., b. Mar. 30, 1799; d. Feb. 13, 1800.

462.....Isaac, Baltimore, Md., b. Oct. 28, 1802; m. Catharine Smith.

463.....Charles, Baltimore, Pa., b. Mar. 25, 1806; d. Sept. 11. 1842.

Family of PETER FORNEY (456) and MARGARET WIEN

464.....Susan Carpenter, Lancaster, Pa., b. Dec. 15, 1815; d. Dec. 10, 1901.

465.....John Wien, Philadelphia, Pa., b. Sept. 30, 1817; d. Dec. 9, 1881; m. Oct. 22, 1839 Matilda Reitzel, b. Sept. 1, 1820; d. Oct. 22, 1898.

Family of JACOB FORNEY (459) and CHRISTIANNA WIEN

465½.....Geo., Lancaster, Pa., b. 1816; d. 1827.

466.....Frederick, Lancaster, Pa., b. 1818; d. 1820.

467.....Charles B., Lebanon, Pa., b. July 18, 1820; d. 1905; m. 1845 Amelia Stehman, b 1819; d. 1879; m. Rachel Pierce.

468.....Sarah, Harrisburg, Pa., b. Jan. 12, 1823; d. Sept. 28, 1847; m. John Lingle.

469.....Wien, Harrisburg, Pa., b. Jan. 30, 1825; d. Jan. 15, 1898; m. 1850 Lydia Gumph, b. May 15, 1824; d. Aug. 29, 1869.

470.....Daniel, Washington, D C., b. Dec. 23, 1827; d. Apr. 13, 1897 m. Catharine Rhinehart.

471.....Jacob, Lancaster, Pa., b. 1829; d. 1865; m. Emma Debolt.

472.....George, Philadelphia, Pa., b. 1831; d. 1895; m. Lizzie Briggs.

Family of ISAAC FORNEY (462) and CATHERINE SMITH

473......George, Baltimore, Pa.
474 ...William, Baltimore, Pa.
475......Isaac, Baltimore, Pa.
476......Amanda, Baltimore, Pa., m. Mr. Reed.
477......Sarah, Baltimore, Pa., m. Mr. Taylor.
478......Susanna, Baltimore, Pa.

Family of JOHN W. FORNEY (465) and MATILDA REITZEL

479......Philip Reitzel, Philadelphia, Pa., b. Dec. 28, 1840; d. July 14, 1872.
480......Gen. James, Philadelphia, Pa., b. Jan. 17, 1844; d. 1920; m. Jeannette de Caines, Richardson, Ky.
481......John Wein, Philadelphia, Pa., b. Aug. 8, 1846; d. May 2, 1893.
482......Mary Stokes, Philadelphia, Pa., b. Nov. 24, 1854· m. H. G. Thunder.
483......Anna Hoover, Philadelphia, Pa., b. Feb. 3, 1858; m. Geo. W. Fitter.
484......Tillie May, Philadelphia, b. May 17, 1862; d. Nov. 1, 1822.

Family of CHARLES B. FORNEY (467) and AMELIA STEHMAN

485......John Stehman, Lebanon, Pa., b. 1846; d. Aug. 8, 1916; m. 1873 Florence Fletcher.
486......Sarah M., Lititz, Pa., b. 1848; d. Aug. 21, 1921.
487......Alice, Lebanon, Pa., b. 1852; d. Dec. 25, 1855.
488......Mary M., Lebanon, Pa., b. 1849; d. Jan. 3, 1856.
489......Deborah, Coleman, Pa., b. 1854; d. Jan. 22, 1862.
490......Charles, Carlisle, Pa., b. Nov. 8, 1856; d. Oct. 1, 1916; m. Elizabeth Rauch, b. 1859; d. 1889; m. Catharine B. Adams, d. July 25, 1916.
491......Sumpter, South Bethleham, Pa., b. Mar. 31, 1861; m. 1890 Susan M. Heisey.

Family of SARAH FORNEY (468) and JOHN LINGLE

492......Infant, Harrisburg, Pa., b.—; d. —.
493......Infant, Harrisburg, Pa. b. —; d. —.

Family of WIEN FORNEY (469) and LYDIA GUMPH

494......Peter William, Washington, D. C., b. Oct. 7, 1851; d. Oct. 27, 1885; m. 1880 Julia A. Grier.
495......Annie F. Chestnut Hill, Philadelphia, Pa., b. May 1, 1853; d. Dec. 13, 1914; m. June 30, 1885 Chancey Brush, b. April 5, 1853; d. Mar. 2, 1911.
496......Clara, Harrisburg, Pa., b. July 9, 1854; d. 1855.
497......Wien, Chicago, Ill., b. Nov. 18, 1862.

Family of DANIEL FORNEY (470) and CATHARINE RHINEHART

498......Emma, Harrisburg, Pa., b. 1854; m. 1877 William H. Eby; d. 1886.
499......Clara, Providence, R. I., b. 1856; m. 1880 Walter J. Comstock, b. Dec. 12, 1853.

Family of JACOB FORNEY (471) and EMMA DEBOLT

500......Michael Wien, Harrisburg, Pa., b. Dec. 1860; m. July 13, 1881 Catharine Preston, b. Aug. 20, 1865.

Family of MICHAEL FORNEY (500) and CATHARINE PRESTON

501......Jacob Charles, Harrisburg, Pa., b. Oct. 21, 1882; m. June 19, 1916 Frances Magee, b. 1885.
502......Emma Kate, Harrisburg, Pa., b. Dec. 16, 1885; m. Charles W. Brown, b. 1885.
503......Nellie Debolt, Harrisburg, Pa., b. July 20, 1885; m. June 27, 1913 Marshall Blair Gourley, b. 1885.
504......Cornelia Frances, Harrisburg, Pa., b. Sept. 1, 1901.

Family of NELLIE DEBOLT FORNEY (503) and MARSHALL BLAIR GOURLEY

505......Doneld Forney, Harrisburg, Pa., b. Feb. 14, 1913.

Family of GEN. JAMES FORNEY (480) and JEANETTE RICHARDSON

506......Angeline, b. —; m. —.
507......Capt. John Wein, b. —; m. Winifred Tait, Oct. 1925, Montreal, Can.

Family of ANNA HOOVER FORNEY (483) and GEO. W. FITTER.

508......George W. Fitter, b. —.

Family of JOHN STEHMAN FORNEY (485) and FLORENCE FLETCHER

509......Fletcher, Lebanon, Pa., b. 1874; m. 1891 Leona Shenk.

Family of CHARLES FORNEY (490) and ELIZABETH RAUCH

511......Amelia Elizabeth, Steelton, Pa., b. 1880; d. 1891.
512......Jacob Griffith, Steelton, Pa., b. May 29, 1882; m. Oct. 7, 1909 Harriet Agnes Wilson.
573......Barbara, Lancaster, Pa., b. April 14, 1884; m. March 28, 1910 Clyde Mylen Herr.
514......Charles W., Carlisle, Pa., b. June 12, 1886.
515......Mary, Carlisle, Pa., b. Jan. 27, 1888; m. Feb. 14, 1907 Morris O. Moore.

Family of CLARA FORNEY (499) and WALTER J. COMESTOCK

516......Comestock, b. —.

Family of JACOB GRIFFITH FORNEY (512) and HARRIET AGNES WILSON

517......Charles Forney, Harrisburg, Pa., b. Aug. 3, 1910.

Family of BARBARA FORNEY (513) and CLYDE M. HERR

518......Benjamin, Lancaster, Pa., May 26, 1911.
519......Charles, Lancaster, Pa., May 10, 1914.
520......Richards Adams, Lancaster, Pa., Feb. 26, 1916.

Inventory of Ann Forney, May 17, 1746, Single

	£	S	d
2 Small Bras Keatles	1	5	
2 Iron pots		8	
A fine Iron 2s 6d gres Pan a Bras	2	4	6
1 8-in. Can		2	
2 Skim Leadels		1	8
A cheamber pot		3	
A Pewter basin & a Leadel		2	
2 Owld Baskets		1	
A Lamp & other Small things		1	
A chair		2	6
A Dung fork and Knif		2	
A Bottle & Jug		1	
Earthenware and trinkary and Pieces Rape		1	6
Testament & other Small Book		1	6
Owld Bags & owld Blankets		1	6
Beading		15	
Wearing apparrall		16	8
Bead steads		8	
Teabell cloths		4	
Bead ceafes		10	
Shifts	1		
Bead sheets		8	
Boulfter and Bed caps		10	
20 yards of Linnen	1	3	
A Pear Skeals and good weights		1	6
An owld chist and an other chist at		15	
Cr for notes and Bonds	77	5	
Cash	14	17	6
Returned 2 June 1746	101	10	10

VIN JAY BRUNIJ
MUSUL WERLSER,
Appraisers.

A True Inventory of the Goods and Effects of Ann Forny Leat Deceased made this 20 day of February 1753 as followeth

	£	S	d
A Peweter tankerd		5	
A Pewter Basan		7	6
Pewter plats Dishes and Basens	1	13	3
A Brass Bukett		10	
2 Iron pots and a Pan		15	
An Owl Keattle		5	
A frein pan 2 Iron Spoans & a flesh fork		7	6
A Cawe	3	0	0
A Mear	8	0	0
Cashe	9	18	3
to out standing Debts by Bond and notes			
Hans Zimerman to a Bond	101	0	0
Martin Hoofman and others to a Bond	122	0	0
Emanuel Carpenter to a Bond	10	15	0
Peter Forney to a note	11	8	0
total Sum	270	4	9

Appraised by
EMANUEL CARPENTER,
HENRY CARPENTER.

A True Inventory of all the goods and Effects of Christian Forney Late deceased made this 3 day of september 1757 as followeth

	£	s	d
To his wearing apparell	6	5	0
15 yards of Druget at 3s per yard	2	5	0
Feather Bead at	5	0	0
to an Owld Sadle and Bridle		10	
to a cutting Boxe		5	
to Grubbing Haws spade	1	0	0
toobs and other simler household goods	3	0	0
Spinny whill 5s an arm chier 3s		8	
to cashe	4		
to out standing Debts per Bonds Notes and Book accounts	198	2	0
to one cawe	2	10	
to a bibell	1		
apreased per as	224	5	0

JON COLES
EMANUEL CARPENTER

A True inventory of the goods and chattles of Abraham Forney of Earl Township Lancaster county and State of Pennsylvania lately Deceased as followeth vis

	£	S	d
one Sorrel Horse	20	0	0
" black mare	19		
" young Black mare	16		
" Bone Horse	18		
" blind Horse	1	2	6
" Black cow	4		
" Brown cow	3	10	
" Brow cow	5	10	
" red cow	4	5	
" Black cow	4		
" red and White Headed cow	4	5	
" Yellow cow	4	10	
" Bull & Black Heaffer	4	10	
2 white and red Spoted Sters	3	0	
2 red Heaffers	2	10	
Thirteen sheep	6	5	
1 wagon	6	10	
Two Harrow	2	5	
one meal chest		7	6
thre dung forks & two Hooks		7	6
Two Grubbig Hows		10	
thre showels and two spades	1	2	6
one Iron sledge and one Crobar	1	0	0
Nineteen cow chans	2	0	0
Six Iron Hay forks		15	
One Wind Mill and three Riddles	2	0	0
one Cutting Bohoc	1		
Two Plows and two Harrows Double trees	3		
all the Horse gears & B	4		
one apple mill	1	10	
one wheel borrow & a Hopple		10	
Two chiszles and three angus & one Drawing Knife		15	
One Grandstone		5	
Six cradles and three Olde siths		7	6
Three Flax Breakers		15	
Four siths and sneaths		10	
one hundred foot of Pine boards		9	
one Sow and five Pigs	2	10	0
three half grow Hogs	2	5	0
Two axes and three weges	1	0	0
Six chairs	1	4	
Puter Dishes plntes and Spoons	3	0	0
one Bross Kettle and one Barl	2	5	

Iron and Brass Ladles and spoons		10	
Four Iron Pots	1		
three Iron Pans and one Baste pr	1		
three little Tubs and six Pails	1		
Ten Panes		7	6
one Butter churn	1	2	6
One Doughtroof and one half Bushel & one Trying Pan		4	6
Three corn Hows		4	6
One Pair Stillyards and one Pair of Scales		15	
one ax and Pinchers one Hammer		10	
one watering can one Teapot one Pair of sheers		5	
one wagon chain and old Iron		10	
one Mans saddle & one Womans Saddle	4		
One coffee mill		7	6
Four tubs	1	10	
The Cider Barrels all	4	0	0
one Doughtrof and Small caske		7	6
One Kitchen Dressor	3		
Two Small casks & one Doughtrof & Earthen Pots		10	
One Clothes Press	1	2	6
One Beds Bedstead	3		
one Bed & Bedstead	7	10	
Four Table clothes		15	
Linon cloth	1	0	0
One Bed and Bedstead	4		
Three Baskets and flox Heckl		10	
Four Table cloths and two peaces of Tow Cloth	1	17	6
Two Peaces of Linsy		15	
yarn and Flax		7	6
Two Chests	1	10	
Two Bedsteads and one Bed	1		
Two Bedstead and one Bed	1	10	
Sole and upper Leather		15	
Three spining wheels and one Big wheel		7	6
Three Tables	2	5	
One Bedstead and one Table	2	12	6
Seven Bags		14	
Two chairs Two Baskets	15	0	0
Four wooden crocks		1	6
One Gun and one carttrige Bokx	1	10	
Two Smoothing Irons and three Brushes Two candle sticks		12	
One Bible and other Books	1	10	
Two Testaments and other Book	1		
Eleven Barrels cider	3	0	0
Two Tea Kettles	2		
Two Bowls and two Bottles and other Small artc	1	2	6

Fity Bushels of Wheat at Six shilling pr bushl	15	0	0
Fifty bushels of Rye three Shilling and nine pence pr bu	5	12	6
First and Second crop Hay	22		
One Promisary Note of Mr. Michael Quiggal due 1885	20		
One Bond of Mr. John Woodhall Due 1786	25	0	0
One Bond of Mr. John Woodhall Due 1788	50		
One Bond of Mr. John Woodhall Due 1787	50		
one Bond Mr. John Woodhall Due 1789	50		
one Bond of Mr. John Woodhal Due 1790	6		
One Bond of Mr. David Orner	30		
Book Debts	19	16	11
Cash	9	11	8
Apraised by John Smith	535	11	7

Emanuel Carpenter
the 20 Jan 1785

Christain Forney)
)Ex
Jacob Carpenter)

WILL OF ABRAM FORNEY

Abraham Forney of Earl Township Lancaster County yeoman being sound in Bedy and mind. Thanks be to God. But remembering the Mortality of My Body, do make hereby this Twenty third Day of January Anna Domine One thousand Seven hundred and Eighty three, this my last wiil and Testament in manner as followeth: To my son Abraham I give devise and bequeath the Tavern on my land near Lancaster Road together with fifteen acres of my Land the line to begin at the west corner of the garden of Said Tavern and thence extending along the Road going from my Tavern to John Carpenters Mill to John Carpenters Line than following John Carpenters line so much as is necessary for said fifteen acres From thence in a straight line to Lancaster Road thence following said Road back to the corner of the Garden then including the House and Garden and joins to the Place of Beginning.

Item I give and devise to him all that Plantation and tract of land which I have bought of Martin Wallison to have and to hold the Said two tracts of lands with all their appertenances. to my son Abraham his heirs and assigns forever under and subject to the incumberances hereafter mentioned and that he shall not take a double share—To my sons John and Peter I give devise and bequeath the Plantation where on I live at present to be divided among them in two Equal Shares according to the Quantity and Quality of the Acres to have and to hold the said Plantation to them their heirs and assigns forever under and subject to all the hereafter mentioned Incumberances. But if any of my said sons should Happen to die without lawful issue then I order his share of land to be divided among my other sons share alike. To my daughter Elizabeth I give and devise a certain Plantation and tract of one hundred and twenty acres and allowances of warrant Land to the same more or less to have and to hold the sd tract of land with all its appertances To my said Daughtor Elizabeth her heirs and assigns under and subject to the Purchase money interest and Quitrent due therefore to the Proprietors these of Situate in Cumberland County near Michael Quickel where she lives at Present

Item I order devise and it is my will that my impotent* son Samuel shall be during the term of his natural life Kept and Maintained by my three sons Abram John and Peter their heirs and assigns and also when he should die be burried by them Decently he must be maintained during life by Equal charges and expenses of my Said three sons Abram John and Peter their heirs or assigns. To my Daughter Maria I give devise and bequeath the sum of one hundred and fifty Pounds Pennsylvania curancy in Specia and to My Daughter Salome I give devise and bequeath the sum of one hundred and fifty Pounds Pensylvania Currancy in spicia the said two Legacies being together three hundred Pounds — I order hereby to be paid to by said three sons their heirs or assigns each paying one third part of said sum. The said my sons shall of said sum pay to said my two Daughters the sum of fifty Pounds when three years after my Death are expired and so forth Every next following year the sum of fifty Pounds until the said two Legacies fully Paid and Satisfied Item I order and it is my will that all my Movable Estate (Excepting my cash Bonds Notes Bills or Book Debts) be divided in four Equal Shares one there of to be given to my wife Elizabeth and to each of my said three sons Abraham Peter and John one equal share there of. Item to my beloved wife Elizabeth I give and devise during the term of her natural life for her Residence the lower stove room and chamber in my Stone Dwelling house a right to the Cellar therein and my said sons Abraham John and Peter shall all her necessary Fire wood delivered before her door well split and each of said My three sons shall pay every year during the term of my wife's natural life unto her the sum of five pounds in specie Money aforesaid and they shall supply her with sufficient meat and Bread all this I give and devise unto her as the full satisfactory for her Dower and she shall have no farther Right to my estate either real or Personal on account of her Dower

Item I order and it is My will that all my cash and other Monies due me by Bonds Bills Notes Book Debts and shall be divided among all My Children and My beloved wife share alike. Finally I hereby ordain and constitude Executors of this my last will and testament my Brother Peter Fahrney and my Dear Brother in law Jacob Carpenter and I hereby impower the said my two executors or any of them then living to grant to any of the said my three sons a good and lawful Conveyance for his share of land which I herein have bequeathed unto him provide they or each of them doth give to them or any of them sufficient security of Necessary for the true performance of all and Every Article by which their lands are Cumbered as aforesaid and all these Conveyances I hereby declare as lawfull as if they were executed by myself in witness where of I have to these presents set my hand and seal the Day and year above written.

Abraham Forney (Seal)

Signed Sealed and
Acknowledged by the testator
to be his last will in the Presence
of us under written witnesses who saw him
Subscribe the Same. John Smith
christian fohrney Jacob Fohrney.

I Abraham Fahrney have this Twenty third Day of November anno one thousand Seven hundred and Eighty four indorsed the following lines as a supplement to this my last will to my son John I bequeath one horse and two cows, to my son Peter bequeath one horse and two cows. Further to these two sons I bequeath

my waggon Plow Harrow and Gears and all grain in the Barn and the field or any where else
to my Daughter Salome I bequeath beside that money which I have given her in my will the sum of twenty Pounds or a horse and a cow which she liketh best my Son Abraham and John must Pay this legacy to my wife Elizabeth besides what I have given to her before I bequeath the two best beds with bed steads and all furniture thereunto belonging and somuch Kitchen and othere Implements as my executors shall think necessary for her use. that article of my movable estate I thought necessary to change I will that all my cash Bonds Notes Book Debts shall be divided among my wife Elizabeth, Abraham John Peter Elizabeth Maria and Salome share alike the rest endue of my movable Estate not bequeathed I bequeath to my three sons Abraham John and Peter to be divided among them share alike in Testamony where of I have put hereunto my hand and Seal

Abraham fourney (Seal)

witness Presant at signing John Smith
Jacob Forney Christian Forney
Lancaster Co. upon tbe twentieth day of January anno Domme 1785 Before me the subscriber personally appeared John Smith Jacob Farney and Christian Fahrney the three subscribing witnesses to the foregoing will and on their solumn afirmation Respectively did declare and say that they were present and saw and heard Abraham Forney the testator therein named sign seal Publish forever and declare the foregoing writing as and for his last will and testament and also codicil to the same to be taken and remain as a part thereof and that at the doing thereof he was of sound mind and well deposing mind Memory and understanding to the best of their Knowledge observation and belief.

James Jacks Reg

Be it Remembered that on the twentieth day of January ano Domme 1785 the last will and Testament together with codicil thereunto of Abraham Fahrney late of Earl township deceased was proved in due form of law and letters Testamony there on were granted to Peter Fahrney and Jacob Carpenter the Executors there in named they having first been duly Qualified well and truly to Adminster the Estate of the said deceased Especially to Exhibit a true and Perfect inventory there of into the Registers office at Lancaster within one months from the date here of and to Render a just and true account of the administration on said Estate within one year or when thereunto lawfully Required given under

James Jacks, Reg

THE IMMIGRANTS AND THEIR DESCENDANTS ON THE OLD HOMESTEAD

The first pioneer of the name Forney who became a permanent yeoman in that part of the country which is now West Earl Township, Lancaster County, Pennsylvania, was Peter Farnia.

There is no definite record obtained when he landed in America but it must have been before the time the demand was made that all male immigrants of the age of sixteen years and over should register in Philadelphia and take the oath of allegiance to the Crown of Great Britain and to the Province of Pennsylvania. His name does not appear in this register nor is the name of his father-in-law, John Smith, recorded in the Pennsylvania Archives, Vol. 17, Second Series which began "PHILD'A YE 18 SEPT'BRE, 1727." Some ship loads including male, female and children were all registered and their ages recorded. The Forneys must have landed at some earlier time, probably as early as 1720.

Traditions gives it that the Smiths, Forneys and Carpenters were always close friends and that they were relatives when in Bern, Switzerland. This we know—they were intimate friends and were very much intermarried in America. There is a belief that they came to Cocalico Creek soon after or with the arrival of Dr. Henry Carpenter to Earl Township. "Rupp's History" gives it that Carpenter came the second time to America accompanied by his family in 1706 and first settled in Germantown, Pa., and came to Lancaster County in 1717. Some of the first settlers squatted on some land and paid a small rent and later made a request for a land grant and survey. There were requests of the above names in this order: Dr. Carpenter for 600 acres on "ye North branch of Contestoga Creek" (Cocalico) June 19, 1726; next record Peter Forney, January 19, 1733, for warrant and survey of 286 acres April 10, 1733 and also warrants and survey for John Smith on the same dates for 300 acres. Carpenter got a warrant on October 31, 1733, survey December 2, 1733 for 1550 acres. Forney got his deed March 13, 1738 for 286 acres and six acres allowances to each hundred acres. These three tracts of land are joining to each other along the Cocalico Creek; the price paid was ten pounds per 100 acres and one shilling quit rent per 100 acres yearly.

There were a number of requests for land in this same vicinity and adjoining these lands that were made in 1717 and 1718 and they received deeds for their land in 1737 so they were living on their land some time before their records appear on the books.

The survey records show a number of adjoining owners' names and all the west side was vacant land at that time and had not been taken up or applied for.

There was an early tradition that three Forney brothers came together to America, one to Lancaster County, one to York County, and the third to Lebanon County but all the geneologists deny the statement as no one was able to reconcile the three names as belonging together.

A brother and two sisters of Peter Forney followed him from Europe, landing in Philadelphia September 23, 1734, in the ship "Hope" which sailed from Rotterdam. The names of the above mentioned persons were Christian, aged 27, Anna Eliza, aged 23, Cathrine, aged 29. Peter Forney was married to Ann, daughter of John Smith and they had two sons and four daughters, Abraham, Peter, Barbara, Anna, Mary and Susan. He built a stone house with a cellar 36 by 44 feet of one story with an attic on the bank of the Cocolico Creek near a spring. A small stone building served as a spring house. After the timber was all cleared from the land the spring ceased to flow in the spring house and it was razed in 1917 but the spring is now small and lower down to the level of the creek. A tradition was handed down the line that Peter and his brother Christian were shearing sheep; one held the sheep and the other did the shearing of the wool. The sheep became unruly and kicked and this caused the shearer to make a miss cut in his hand and this gave rise to a quarrel between the brothers. One of them started to run and the other threw the shears after him but the battle soon ended and they repented of their anger toward each other, "made up" again and then said, "Ya, ye, das Switzer Blude hut sich gereckt." By this expression we would conclude that they came from Switzerland. Earlier however, they must have come from near Geneva in Province Ain in France. There is a town by the name Ferney in that country which must have derived its name from the inhabitants with the same appellation. These people left this town about 1685 when the king signed the revocation of the Edict of Nantes so they fled under the persecution as they were Hugenots.

The following is a quotation from tracings of the ancestral lines by Mrs. Annie Forney Brush. "And now we may mention tradition and some certain facts from which we may speculate. A great, great grand-daughter of Peter Forney has told the writer (A. F. B.) many times that her great aunts told her that the Forneys came from that part of France which is near Geneva. They further were careful to impress upon her that the Forneys were people of some importance in the old country. In a sketch of the Forney family of North Carolina in Wheeler's History of that state we learn that they were Hugenots; the General Peter and Abraham Forney who served in the Revolution War came from that family and the Hugenot extraction is stated in the account of him in Appleton's Cyclopedia of America biography in a local history read by the writer when she was in Geneva. There is an interesting account of a Protestant gentleman, Pierre Chevalier De Ferney, who lived in the modest chateau afterwards owned by Voltaire and whose family left France and fled into Germany at the time of the great Hugenot exodus. The late John W. Forney of Philadelphia, when he was in Paris in 1875 met a Monsieur Forney who, judging by the number of letters which he wrote and the contents of the same read by the writer, seemed anxious to claim relationship. He writes among other things that he was from Geneva and that he was sure that the Americans Forneys would be glad to hear what he had to tell of the family. Whether the meeting ever took place is not known. Monsieur Forney died a few years afterwards and left his fortune to found a library and a school in Paris. The letters just mentioned were sent to a Carpenter cousin. The writer asked why they were sent to a Carpenter and was informed that the Carpenters and Forneys were related in the old country."

Jacob Forney, the ancestor of the Southern Forneys, first came to America on the ship "Friendship" and qualified September 3, 1739 being then 18 years of age. See Penna. Archives Vol. 17, Sec. Series P. 192. He remained some years and returned to his old home to procure his legacy of his deceased ancestors and returned to America on the ship "St. Andrews," and qualified in Philadelphia on September 23, 1752. See Penna. Archives Vol. 17 P. 357, Sec. Series. He was "registered as sick." Tradition gives it that there was a love story enacted while he was sick aboard. A rosy-cheeked, buxom girl, Maria Bergman, a passenger on the same ship nursed him and this friendship resulted in a marriage soon after the ship landed. Some think that he was a relative of Peter Forney as he and his wife remained two years in the Cocalico Creek district, Lancaster County and in 1754 went on a journey to Lincoln County, North Carolina and on this journey he stopped and visited John Adam Forney at Digg's Choice now Hanover, York County, Pa. The General Peter and Abraham Forney mentioned in Annie F. Bush's notes were sons of this Jacob Forney.

Ann, a sister of Peter Forney died single in 1746.

Of Cathrine, also a sister, no further record is obtained.

Christian, a brother, lived in Warwick Township and it is believed that he was a tanner by occupation as there were some tan vats and wooden water mains on Peter Forney's farm across the Cocalico Creek, northwest of the wooden covered bridge, now a cement concrete bridge in Warwick township. He died in 1757 and his will mentions his wife Elizabeth heir to all his possessions.

Peter Forney died in 1747 and had made no will so his personal property was appraised on July 31, 1749 as £119, 8s.0d and remained intact in his wife's possession until she died and was then appraised on February 20, 1753 at £270 .4s .9d. She gave in her will to her minor daughters Mary and Susan £10 each and the balance was equally divided among all of her children. The real estate had been appraised on the fifth day of September 1749 by Gabrael Carpenter, Rudy Stone, John Landus and Jacob Sensime. The 286 acres with two buildings thereon were appraised at £570 0s. 0d. and the 75 acres rough ground granted by patent to John Smith, his wife's share at £80. 0s. 0d, being in the whole six hundred and fifty pounds or about $8.25 per acre. The confirmation of the deed took place on the 12th of December 1754. The children had an equal share of the proceeds excepting Abraham, the oldest son according to law took a double share. The entire tract was transferred to Abraham Forney who then sold 177 acres to his brother Peter Forney and he then built a stone house and other farm buildings. The farm is now owned by Milton Royer, Lancaster, Pa.

Abraham Forney built a hotel at the cross road corner of the Lancaster, Reading and Newport road in 1765 which was part of the 75 acres, the tract of the Smith patent. The Inn was noted far and wide and was known as Forney's "Wertzhouse." Our ancestors have made statements that the hotel was kept and known as a well preserved and respectable public house and was handed down from one generation to another comprising four generations or one hundred and eight years. After the death of Abraham Forney, the first proprietor, the only "drinkable" that appeared on the inventory list of the appraisement was about twenty-five barrels of cider but by this we do not mean to say that cider was the sole "wet goods" sold as there was usually a supply of whisky, brandy, rum, gin and wine on hand. Tradition gave it that the "tipers" of the community came there one evening for the purpose of drinking the "Wertzhouse Drucke". They continued until late into the night. The proprietor had to go to the cellar to refill the bottles and remained sometime to collect the odds and ends of liquor. When he came up from the cellar he was asked why he lingered so long and he replied that he had to roll a new barrel on the lager and tap it. The drinkers then agreed to have one drink more from the new barrel and return home since they could not carry out their purpose to "drink the place dry." This was one of the proprietor's jokes for on the next morning there was not a whole quart of whisky on hand.

Abraham Forney, the oldest son of Peter and Ann Smith Forney was born about 1720. He was married to Elizabeth, daughter of Jeremiah Spurgeon, and had four sons and three daughters.

He was a soldier in the Revolutionary War with three of his sons, Abraham, John and Peter. The court records at Lancaster states that he was constable in 1765 and having appeared at the regular term of court in November, stayed long enough to answer the roll and then afterwards absented himself without permission. He was fined ten shillings along with twelve other delinquents. While he served in the war the women were the bar tenders, a service which was not uncommon in those days. After the war the oldest son, Abraham, kept the hotel and the father looked after his farm assisted by his second son, John He died four years after he was mustered out of the Continental Army and left a large estate. The appraisement of his personal property was £535. 1s. 7d. Among this list was his apparel appraised at £15, so from this we would imagine that he had some fine clothing. In his will he gave the hotel and farms to the three oldest sons. One farm however, in Cumberland County, of 120 acres he gave to his daughter, Elizabeth, who was married to Michael Quigley. In the division of property Abraham received the hotel farm and John the homestead farm and Peter was paid his share by his brothers and went into mercantile business handling grain and flour, also speculating in the buying and selling of farms, a speculation which was very risky from 1810 to 1820. He was caught in the "slump" of values of farm land and failed and in 1820 appointed as his assignees his brother, John Forney and his son Emanuel Forney. But before the estate was settled his brother died and his son, Emanuel, moved to Lebanon County, Pa., and the estate was then settled by his nephew, Levi Forney, and it paid out .33542 per cent. He never recovered financially and he was later supported by his nephews and died at the home of Levi Forney in 1837. His wife was Ann ...., and his children were Peter, Emanuel, Catharine, Hannah and Sallie. The writer had seen the last two girls when a small boy. The oldest son disappeared from his home and nothing was afterwards heard from him nor was there ever any revelation as to his fate.

Abraham, oldest son of Abraham, remained at the hotel and continued farming. He married Ann Maria Weidman and had two sons and one daughter, John W., Abraham and Catharine. Abraham was known intimately as "Big Abe". He was married to Lydia Levan.

John, second son of Abraham, was married to Elizabeth, daughter of Daniel Lehman of Pequea. She could speak English fluently and was known as the most beautiful married woman in all Earl Township. She was of medium height and rather light weight, was quite active and had her rosy, cheeks and smiling face in her eighties. An uncle of the writer told him that she wore gay clothing and this uncle visited much at her home when a small boy (she being his grandmother) and at evening when she put him to bed she always taught him to say his prayers.

Samuel, the impotent son of Abraham, was a very bright boy and young man and of great physical strength. At the age of nineteen, one very hot day he was pitching hay in the meadow and when he was very much over heated he came to a spring of cold water and plunged into it. This chilled his blood and brought on a brain storm and afterwards he was subject to some sort of "spells" He was aware of this weakness and so when he felt a "spell" coming on he would ask to be tied and locked to a special ring that was placed in the upstairs especially for this purpose. In this way he would do no harm, neither to himself nor to any other person. He was supported by his older brothers as was stipulated in his father's will.

Elizabeth married Michael Quickel and lived on the farm she received as her share from her father's estate in Cumberland County, Pa., but the location of the farm is now on Cocolamas Creek in Juinata County, which was then a part of Cumberland County.

Maria and Salome remained single.

John remained on the home farm and had two sons and one daughter. His oldest son, John, was married to a first cousin of his, Catharine, daughter of Abraham and Maria Weidman Forney. When he was but fourteen years of age he was driving a four horse team and a large Conestoga covever wagon, hauling wheat and flour to Philadelphia and bringing back merchandise in return. After his marriage he was having a hotel at Earlville which is now Talmage. His second son, Levi, was first married to Lydia Keller who died the first year after her marriage. Levi afterwards married Maria Rupp, daughter of Abraham Rupp and Elizabeth Kurtz. He lived on the farm until 1849 at which time he sold it. His entire family was born on the homestead. He intended to move to Virginia so with three of his sons he drove to Virginia in a carriage and there made a contract for a farm. However, after returning home one of the sons persuaded him not to take the Virginia land and so he forfeited the money he had paid on it and then bought a fine farm near Lititz and there reared his family. His sons all remained farmers with the exception of John, who was a cattle dealer. The first five generations were practically all farmers. In the first four generations in the line of the oldest son not one became a member of any church organization. They were a law-abiding and quiet, peaceable people. They were God-fearing and revered Him, observing the returning of thanks before partaking of their meals. They owned Bibles and Testaments as appears in the inventory and appraisal of their goods.

The sons of Abraham Forney to the fourth generation were heavy and tall in stature. John W. and his brother Abraham, who was more particularly known as "Big Abe" were especially well built. John W. was six feet, three inches and Abe must have been some taller.

Abraham Forney was married to Lydia Levan and moved to Schafferstown, Pa., and was there having a hotel and only reached the age of thirty-seven years. His widow was his only survivor.

John W. Forney married Barbara B. Baker and remained on the father's place and continued the hotel business during the remainder of his life. He had been buying and selling considerable real estate and was also quite successful dealing in cattle. During the summer and fall season he would go west and bring from there herds of cattle and sell them to the farmers for winter feeding and then in the spring he would buy them again and take them to the Philadelphia market. In those days the cattle had to be transported by foot in large herds as there were no railroads. Travel then was by stage coach, carriage, horseback and much by walking.

John W. had three sons and six daughters. William, his oldest son was married to Catharine Graybill and he had a hotel at "Fiddler's Green" now known as Neffsville. William Forney had one son and one daughter. The son, Graybill Forney, when he reached manhood was also having a hotel in Earlville now known as Talmage, for fourteen years. His remains are in the Carpenter cemetery.

In the line of Abraham Forney of the third generation there are no male members living by the name Forney and only two girls who were born in the Forney name so in that line the name became extinct.

JOHN W. FORNEY

BARBARA BAKER FORNEY

THE HOTEL REBUILT

HOTEL BARN

ABRAHAM B. FORNEY

Abraham B. Forney, one of the three sons of John W. and Barbara Baker Forney, was born September 26, 1809, and was married March 21, 1837 to Mary Lane, born May 18, 1809. Mr. Forney moved to Willow Glen Farm, near Riverton, Warren County, Virginia, some years prior to the Confederate outbreak of war. He lived on Winchester Pike or main road where the Northern and Southern armies would pass on their offensive and defensive marches and several times was between the two armies in their skirmishes or battles. On these occasions he was advised by an officer to take his family in the chimney corner or cellar and remain there until the guns ceased firing and danger was over.

Mr. Forney always told the generals of either army that he was a Union man and a staunch Republican from the Old Whig party for which Lancaster County, Pa., always was and is now famous, and that he could not divert from that as he had some real estate interest in Lancaster County. He was always respected by the generals of the Southern army and treated with more consideration by them than by the Yankees though the same hospitality was meted out to both armies alike. During the encampment of an army near his home the official staff seemed always to be entertained in his home so that he was on speaking terms with both sides and did enjoy the fellowship of each one at different times. This was truly a unique situation for one whose sympathy was with the Union. The feature that saved him "bodily" was that he always told the truth and from the beginning to the end always told one and the same story. On one occasion his vote was refused because of high sentiment existing at that particular time. But after making a speech and telling the crowd assembled what a true American was and that this was the land of the brave and free, Mr.Forney was tapped on the shoulders, called"a good citizen" and told to vote as he pleased. Besides his vote there were six others polled in the county at this date "solid Republicans."

On the last Southern campaign coming north Mr. Forney's property was all destroyed except the house. His barns, saw-mill, brick manufacturing buildings and lime sheds were all burned. This was done by the stragglers of the Southern army and was contrary to the wishes of the head generals. In the destruction of his pig pens the pigs began to run and he had some Chester Whites imported from Lancaster County, Pa., and these white ones made good targets in the night and none escaped excepting a few black ones. In one of the campaigns they stole most of Mrs. Forney's chickens and after they were gone by she gathered up the remaining chickens and placed them on the garret of her large house and fed them there. Then after some defeat the army was retreating and in passing by Mr. Forney's house a rooster that was among the hens crowed and the soldiers having heard it went into the house and up to the attic and took all of Mrs. Forney's precious, stowed away chickens.

When the army was marching north they told Mr. Forney that they were going into his country to get some fat cattle from the Pennsylvania Dutch Yankees, he thereupon told them to be careful or they would come back with a bee in their ears. When defeated and on their return they said: "Ah! You can't grip the Dutch."

June first to the fourteenth in 1863, marks the time when Gen. R. H. Millroy and ten thousand men holding Winchester. Col. A. F. McReynolds and his cavalry scouts patroled the valley as far as Front Royal. The Front Royal road from Winchester passes by Mr. Forney's farm and through Riverton. The 12th Pennsylvania cavalry in charge of Lieut.-Col. Moss, to the number of four hundred strong went out and returned with the report that they had been stopped by a rebel force. Gen. Millroy refused to credit the story insisting that they had been too easily frightened and that if any such force could be there he should have heard of its approach from Gen. Hooker or Gen. Halleck. Nevertheless, he advised McReynolds to look carefully. Next morning (June 13, Saturday), however, his patrols on the Front Royal road reported the enemy advancing in large forces whereupon Gen. Millroy signaled McReynolds to join him while he sent out a considerable force on either road to learn what was "brewing." Gen. Millroy was in command in the Shenandoah Valley under Gen. Schenck as department commander at Baltimore. On June 12 (Friday) some of Gen. Millroy's army were in hard pressed quarters at Riverton on the Front Royal road and the night being dark they did not know the way out so they called on Mr. Forney at midnight to pilot them through Manassas Gap out of danger from the pursuing rebel forces. He made an excuse that it might cost him his life but this availed nothing. They put him on a horse and he led the army through the mountain pass on the darkest of nights. "Thank you" was his reward, and with his breath in his throat he returned to his home the next morning on his horse. Some neighbors having seen him said: "Why Mr. Forney, where have you been so early this morning?" He answered: "I piloted the Yankees." Of course this was a dreadful thing to do in the hot bed of the Rebellion and they threatened to hang him or punish him severely but it all bridged over and no harm was done to him. Some hooted at him, "Ha! ha! Mr. Forney, you think for the favor you did for them, in return, when you get to Washington, they will give you anything you ask."

After the war ended Mr. Forney put in a claim to the government for an amount of about twenty-five thousand dollars to cover the loss of his destroyed property but to this date no allowances have been made. Some people say that the heirs will get it some day!

During this time Mrs. Forney went North to Lancaster County, Pennsylvania, being accompanied by her daughter, Emaline, who was then about eight years of age. She had a pass from the Union General to pass through the picket lines. They walked from Winchester to Martinsburg, a distance of twenty-two miles. Emaline's dress had some fancy decorations on the shoulders and she was advised to take this off lest it would attract attention and make them conspicuous in passing through the enemy's lines. Dearly as she loved this frock Miss Emaline complied with the officer's request and only in years afterwards could she forgive but it was hard to forget. While in Lancaster County, Mrs. Forney heard a rumor that her husband had been shot and of course to substantiate the rumor she hurried home only to find him sitting on the veranda of his house peacefully smoking a cigar.

Some years after the war, Mr. Forney sold his Virginia farms as he had fallen heir to the old hotel and farm from his father's estate, in Lancaster County, Pennsylvania. He did not like the hotel business and in 1873 sold the form of 55 acres with a two story (part stone and part frame) Tavern which was erected by his great grandfather, Abraham Forney in 1765, together with the stone gable bank barn built by his father, John W. Forney in 1822 to Jacob L. Erb and whose heirs in 1888 conveyed the property to Daniel R. Brackbill. On July 17, 1908 the old hotel was destroyed by fire. It was soon rebuilt by a frame structure on the same foundation and a picture is shown in this book of the present hotel and barn located on the corners of Lancaster, Reading and Newport road intersection.

Mr. and Mrs. Forney had a family of ten children but only one lived to attain womanhood. The parents lived to the advanced ages of eighty-five and eighty-one years respectfully. Their remains were laid to rest in the grave yard on the old Lane farm adjoining Lane's church between Neffsville and Oregon.

The only descendants now living are the two daughters and the one son of the late Walter Johns and his wife Emaline Forney, namely Miss Mary Lane Johns, Virginia, wife of John F. Nissley, and children, Virginia Johns and Mary Dell, and Walter Johns, all of Lancaster, Pa.

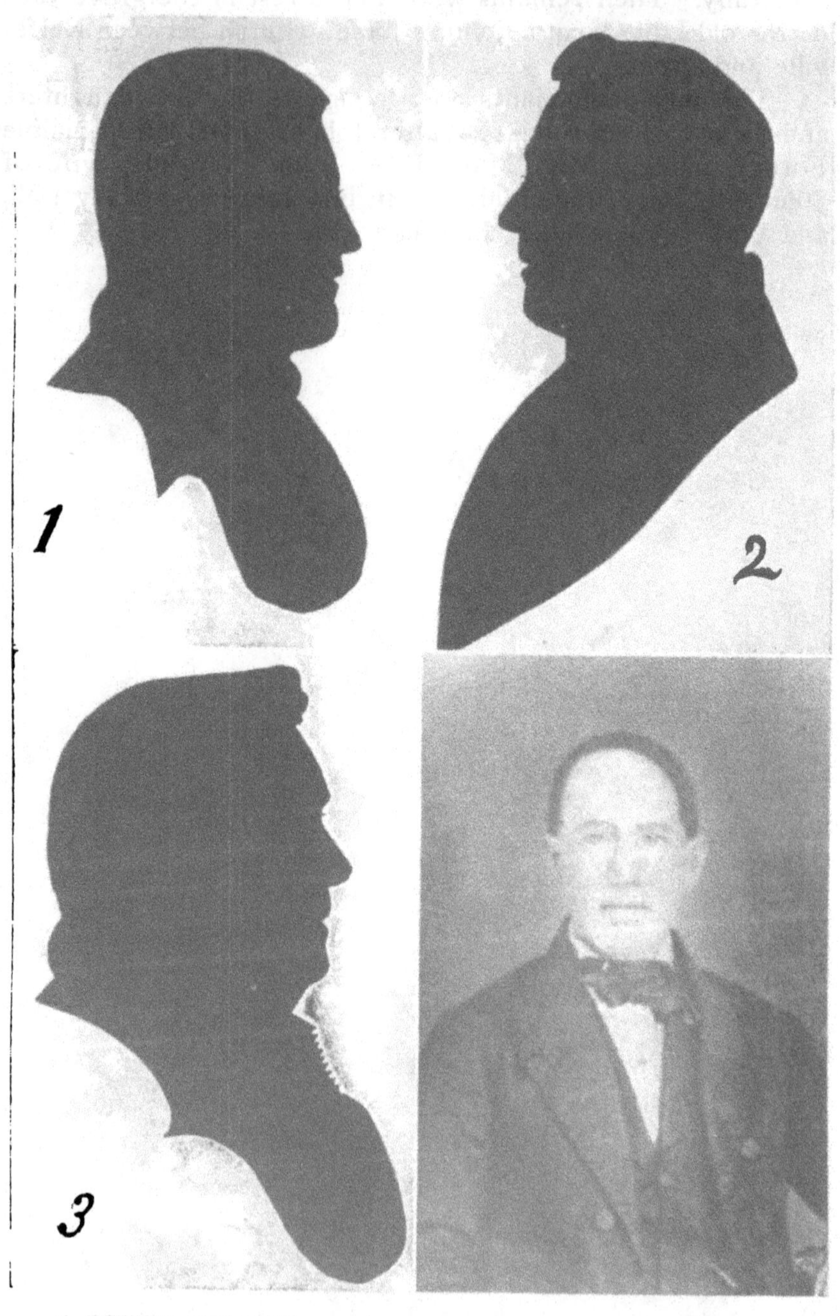

1 PETER FORNEY 2 ABRAHAM FORNEY

3 JOHN FORNEY 4 LEVI FORNEY

ABRAHAM R. FORNEY SALINDA F. HERTZLER
ANNA H. YOUNG
NAOMI Y. RUHL CHESTER Y. RUHL

ABRAHAM R. FORNEY JOHN K. FORNEY
E. H. FORNEY
FRANCES LEON LITTLE MARTHA LOUISE LITTLE

THE FAMILY OF LEVI FORNEY

Levi Forney reared his family on the new homestead near Lititz. In this family we find that all the children became members of some church organization with the exception of one who remained single and died at middle age. The oldest son was a member of the Mennonite church and the remainder were all affiliated with the Brethren church formerly known as Dunkards.

Levi Forney's remains were laid away at the cemetery of Erb's church in Penn Township, Lancaster County, Pa.

In the sixth generation we find some leaving the farms and following other occupations, and we also find one of them a minister of the Gospel and in the seventh generation we find several more became ministers.

All the children of Levi Forney remained and were occupied on the farms raising farm products, and a number of them were regular attendants at the Lancaster product market. They were all prosperous and built up for themselves comfortable homes. They were all married excepting one who was engaged in the cattle trading business, and remained in his father's home and died there. His remains were placed in the Erb's cemetery in Penn Township.

JOSEPH R. FORNEY

REV. PHARAS J. FORNEY

REV. ROY S. FORNEY

REV. MILTON G. FORNEY

JOSEPH G. FORNEY

THE FAMILY OF JOSEPH G. FORNEY

Joseph G. Forney, of Lancaster, is now one of the foremost men of the day in that city and county, his extensive activities in real estate and insurance and his prominence in the world of finance placing him as an outstanding figure in the city affairs of Lancaster. Levi Forney, grandfather of Joseph G. Forney, was born on the homestead, but later in life removed to Penn township and there established this branch of the family. Joseph R. Forney, father of J. G. Forney, was born on the original homestead near Brownstown, removing to Penn township in his boyhood, with the family. He became a thrifty and successful farmer, and reared thirteen children to whom he was devoted, eight of whom are now living. He died in 1908 at the age of seventy-four years.

Joseph G. Forney was born at the homestead in Penn township, July 24, 1876. His elementary education was acquired in the district public school, and he later attended the Millersville Normal school, completing his studies with a special course at the Perkiomen Seminary, at Pennsburg, which he finished in 1901. After teaching school for a few years, Mr. Forney spent several years in the west, acting as branch manager for the Geiser Manufacturing Company, first at Indianapolis, Indiana, then being transferred to Lincoln, Nebraska, thence to Kansas City, Missouri, and finally to Louisville, Kentucky, returning to Lancaster in 1907. Mr. Forney opened an office on January first of that year, establishing his present business in real estate and insurance. Early advancing to the front rank in his chosen field, he has developed a business which is one of the most important in that part of the state.

In various branches of organized endeavor Mr. Forney is a leader of progressive activities. He is secretary of the Board of the Directors of the Agricultural Trust and Savings Company of Lancaster, one of the leading financial institutions of the County. For a number of years he has also been a director of the Lancaster Chamber of Commerce, having been elected President of this organization in 1925. He is also President of the Lancaster Real Estate Board and an efficient worker for its growth and progress. He is secretary of the Federal Exchange Automobile Insurance Company of Reading, Pa., and for thirteen years he has been secretary of the Lancaster Automobile Club of Lancaster, Pa., and is a member of the Kiwanis Club of Lancaster.

Fraternally, he is a member of all the Masonic bodies up to the thirty-second degree and his clubs are the Hamilton, Country and Shrine of Lancaster, serving the last named as President.

THE FAMILY OF ABRAHAM R. FORNEY

ABRAHAM R. FORNEY AND WIFE
At the Age of 50 Years

Abraham R. Forney was born in West Earl Township on the old Forney homestead, January 23, 1827. He was reared on this farm. He spent part of his boyhood fishing in the Cocalico Creek and he often related stories of these times in the later days of his life.

When a small boy he had a regular weekly errand carrying a loaf of bread to an old Indian who had a hut built in the woodland across the creek at the northwest part of the farm. His grandmother always baked an extra loaf for the Indian, and Aby than take it to him.

He was married May 14, 1846, in Lancaster, to Anna Keller and the following year he rented a farm of one hundred and forty acres in West Donegal Township on which farm he spent thirty-nine years as a renter. In 1886 he made sale of his farming implements and stock and bought a home in Elizabethtown, Pa., and lived there in a retired life. A few years later he bought the farm he had lived on from the Gross estate.

Mr. Forney was a school director in West Donegal Township. He was one of the organizers of the Elizabethtown Exchange Bank which institution was organized in 1887 and at which time he served as director and vice-president of the institution and later was elected its president.

Mr. Forney was a well preserved man and reached the age of eighty-two years. At his death his body was placed in the family lot at Mount Cemetery by the side of his wife, who had died eight years before.

THE FAMILY OF JOHN K. FORNEY

ANNIE S. HOFFMAN AND J. K. FORNEY
Time of Marriage, Age 23

J. K. Forney was born December 1, 1850, in West Donegal Township, Lancaster County, Pennsylvania. He spent his boyhood and young manhood days on the farm, which is characteristic of some of our most prominent and successful business men. For a few months each winter he availed himself of the advantages of the public school education at

Pleasant Hill School, West Donegal Township, Lancaster County. This was the only educational opportunity afforded him and the curriculum of this school was very limited in those days offering only a few branches of study which were spelling, reading, writing, geography and arithmetic.

Mr. Forney, as a boy remained at his home with his parents, visiting the grand parents twice a year. Until the age of twenty he was outside of Lancasted County only four times, at those times making trips to Harrisburg, Reading, Lebanon and the river hills of York County. At the age of twenty he made a trip west, going as far as Chicago. This was the same year of the great fire. On this same trip he also visited St. Louis. There was then no bridge there to cross the Mississippi River, the first piers for the Eads bridge being then in construction. Mr. Forney returned home the fall of that year, went to school part of the winter and again went west the next summer visiting Chicago and seeing what remained intact and the balance in ruins and ashes. This time he returned home during corn harvesting period. The following winter he went to the mountain districts working at the construction of railroads. He also assisted as a mechanic in the Round House, at Renova, Pa. The following year he was home on the farm with his parents and was married to Annie S. Hoffman on October 2, 1873. In 1874 he began farming, making a specialty of marketing at Marietta and Columbia until the spring of 1879. At that time he and his family moved to Kansas where in 1878 he had purchased a farm. There as a Pennsylvania farmer he tilled the Kansas soil. His chief concern was his individual home making and prosperity. Upon his arrival he began to build a house and later a good barn and other buildings to shelter his flocks. He remained on the farm eleven years and in addition to his farming he operated a steam threshing outfit for eight years and two years he used horse power.

While on the farm the cows increased and the butter and the eggs were taken to the stores in Abilene to get in trade provisions and goods and the credit balance increased above that of the needs and so these farmers began to look for a different outlet. One hot day in August, 1885, in the shade of a box-elder tree was held a meeting attended by J. E. Nissley, Eli and Christian Hoffman, N. G. Hershey and J. K.

Forney. All of these men had been identified with the dairy in Lancaster County and they decided to have Mr. J. K. Forney make an investigation of the creameries when he should visit his home place in Lancaster County, Pa., which visit took place in the winter of 1885 and 1886.

The following is a quotation from the Kansas City, Mo., Journal, November 26, 1916; "And to repeat J. K. Forney's story of his impression of those pioneer Lancaster County creameries which led him into near doubt whether a large industry could ever be built with their meager equipment as a foundation would require an interesting chapter all by itself." The impression was this. One cold, almost zero weather, morning he took a two mile walk through the snowy fields to a creamery and the milk was slow in coming in but finally the separator was started and the cream came out of the spout in a thread about the size of a straw so that it took a long time to cover the bottom of the vat. By inquiring from some who were in the business and who had made a failure of it Mr. Forney arrived at the "near doubt" stage referred to in the Kansas City paper. However, Mr. Forney returned to Abilene and a second meeting was held by the same parties mentioned above and they started their little plant on November 24, 1886 at Belle Springs, Kansas, twelve miles southeast of Abilene. Mr. Forney moved from his farm October 20, 1889 to Abilene. By this time they had built a new and somewhat larger plant in Abilene into which industry he put all his energy. First he worked as an assistant and later as a butter maker. In 1894 he was made secretary and manager which office he held until 1899 when his son Elmer H. Forney took the management of the creamery. Mr. J. K. Forney was later elected president, which office he still holds. To the original creamery building were added new buildings in 1902 and completed in 1903 and also in 1906 and 1908. The business has grown to include poultry and eggs, the manufacture of ice cream and ice and the establishment of a cold storage plant and poultry feeding plant.

Mr. Forney has been visiting much in his time. In the interest of his business and for various other reasons he has been in all of the forty eight states of the Union. He has crossed the Rocky Mountains eleven times and the Alleghenies more than forty times. He also made a trip around the world going eastward. In that year he traveled thirty-five thousand miles, twenty-four thousand miles by water and eleven thousand miles on land. He traveled six thousand miles in India at an expense of $39.40 for the railroad ticket. His entire cost for the year's travel was $532.40 which amount included ship and car fare, hotel and incidental expenses amounted to about $500.00. This trip was made in the winter of 1898 and 1899.

JOHN K. FORNEY AND WIFE
At the Age of 48 Years

The year 1901 marks Mr. Forney's first visit to the old Forney homestead which they received from the Penns, the proprietors of the state of Pennsylvania. He then began to search for record and dates of the early Forney immigrants and to arrange the same into a book of genealogy together with history obtained from records and some from tradition. In the research he found that two Forney families lived in Lancaster County in the years shortly after 1723 but no definite time could be obtained of their landing. In his own line was Peter Forney who lived on the banks of the Cocalico Creek in Earl Township and the other was John Forney who died April 1769 but who also lived on the banks of the Cocalico Creek in Cocalico Township near Reamstown.

All the descendants of these families have gone from this locality and from Mr. Forney's ancestors it was handed down that these two families of Forneys were no relatives.

In civic affairs Mr. Forney was one of the first water commissioners of the city of Abilene and also served as utility commissioner at the time when Abilene started on the commission form of government. He was always interested in helping to improve the city for the good of his fellow men. He was also elected one of the trustees of the Abilene Cemtry Association of which organization he is a member at this writing.

At the age of twenty-seven he became a believer in the Lord Jesus Christ as his personal Savior through the merits of His atoning blood that was shed on the cross for whosoever will accept Him. He has been a member of the Brethren in Christ church earlier known as the River Brethren. This is his testimony copied from a paper in his old Bible: "The offering and sacrifice on the Cross, God has accepted as a sweet smelling savour and the proof of its acceptance is furnished to angels, men and devils in the fact that God has raised Him from the dead. Nothing can be added to the efficiency of that atoning sacrifice. Nothing can be added to the completeness of that finished work. Nothing can be added to the value of that precious blood. Any attempt to add something of our own in the way of feelings, repentance, good resolutions, charitable deeds or ecclesiastical ordinances that salvation may be rendered more certain and secure is an insult to God and a dishonor to the Lord Jesus Christ and a grief to the Holy Spirit. Repentance, faith, a new birth and holiness; these are all great and glorious gifts all purchased by the blood divine for which I adore and praise a triune God, still none of them atoned for my sins. Repentance did not die for me; faith did not die for me; holiness did not die for me; my confidence is not in the gift but in Giver—the eternal Son of God who took my nature as my substitute and in that atoned for my sins. On his finished work alone does my soul rely for pardon, holiness and heaven and He only is made unto me wisdom, righteousness, sanctification and redemption."

J. K. FORNEY

ABRAM H. FORNEY

Abram H. Forney was a veteran in the World War in the 110 Engineers and being in a number of battles and sieges in France. Charles W. Forney of Carlisle, Pa., and Capt. John Wein Forney, son of General James Forney of Philadelphia, were also in service.

FAMILY OF E. H. FORNEY

Elmer H. Forney was born in West Donegal Township, Lancaster County, Pennsylvania, November 19, 1875.

He came with his parents to Kansas, arriving at Abilene March 28, 1879 and lived on a diary farm on Turkey Creek near Belle Springs, southeast of Abilene, until October 20, 1889, after which date he came with his parents to Abilene, Kansas.

Attended grade schools and finished first year in high school in Abilene.

During vacation of school years was employed as grocery clerk, delivery boy and bookkeeper in retail grocery store.

At the age of nineteen years was employed by the Belle Springs Creamery Company as bookkeeper and four years later succeeded his father as secretary and manager of same company.

On November 20, 1898 was married to Hannah Lois Nutt of Abilene, Kansas.

Was active in civic organizations in the community; member of the Lutheran church, and a thirty-second degree Mason.

THE BELLE SPRINGS CREAMERY COMPANY

Abilene, Kansas

J. K. Forney, President, E. H. Forney, General Manager

COL. JOHN W. FORNEY

JOHN WEIN FORNEY

John Wein Forney, an American journalist and politician, was born at Lancaster, Pennsylvania, on September 30, 1817. He was apprenticed to a printer in Lancaster, Pennsylvania in 1833. In 1840 he published the Intelligencer and Journal of that city, a Democratic paper and in 1845 he became surveyor of the port of Philadelphia and was editor of the Pennsylvanian, a paper published in Philadelphia. From 1851 to 1855 he was clerk of the House of Representatives at Washington, D. C., and in 1856 was elected chairman of the Pennsylvania Democratic state committee. In 1859 he was again elected clerk of the House of Representatives and in 1861 became secretary of the United States Senate. In 1871-72 he became collector of the city of Philadelphia. He was editor of the Washington Union in 1851, of the Philadelphia Press in 1857, of Washington Chronicle in 1859, and of Progress, a weekly journal published in Philadelphia, in 1879. He died in Philadelphia December 9, 1881 and his remains are buried in the Laurel Hill cemetery, Philadelphia, Pa.

WORKS FULL TIME HELPING CARPENTER

SARAH ANN STAUFFER

Meet the only feminine carpenter's helper in the world.

Sarah Ann Stauffer, 9-year-old daughter of Mr. and Mrs. Charles F. Stauffer, 327 East Orange street, dons overalls each morning, reports forwork promptly at 7 o'clock and receives a pay envelope on Saturday. She works for her father.

The contents of the envelope goes to a fund for a new bicycle and pin money for a trip to the sea shore.

Sarah Ann with a soiled nose paused in her labors at the remodeling operations at 115 North Queen street this morning long enough to pose for the camera man. Her fathersays she is very useful in the light work to be done about the building. It is Sarah Ann's second summer in the building construction business.

(From Lancaster Intelligencer, July 18, 1925.)

MARY LANE JOHNS

Self-named "Gypsy Maid" made a tour through the Mediterranean Sea, Holy Land and Egypt and in an airship from Paris to London. Quite brave.

LEVI R. FORNEY

MARTIN K. FORNEY

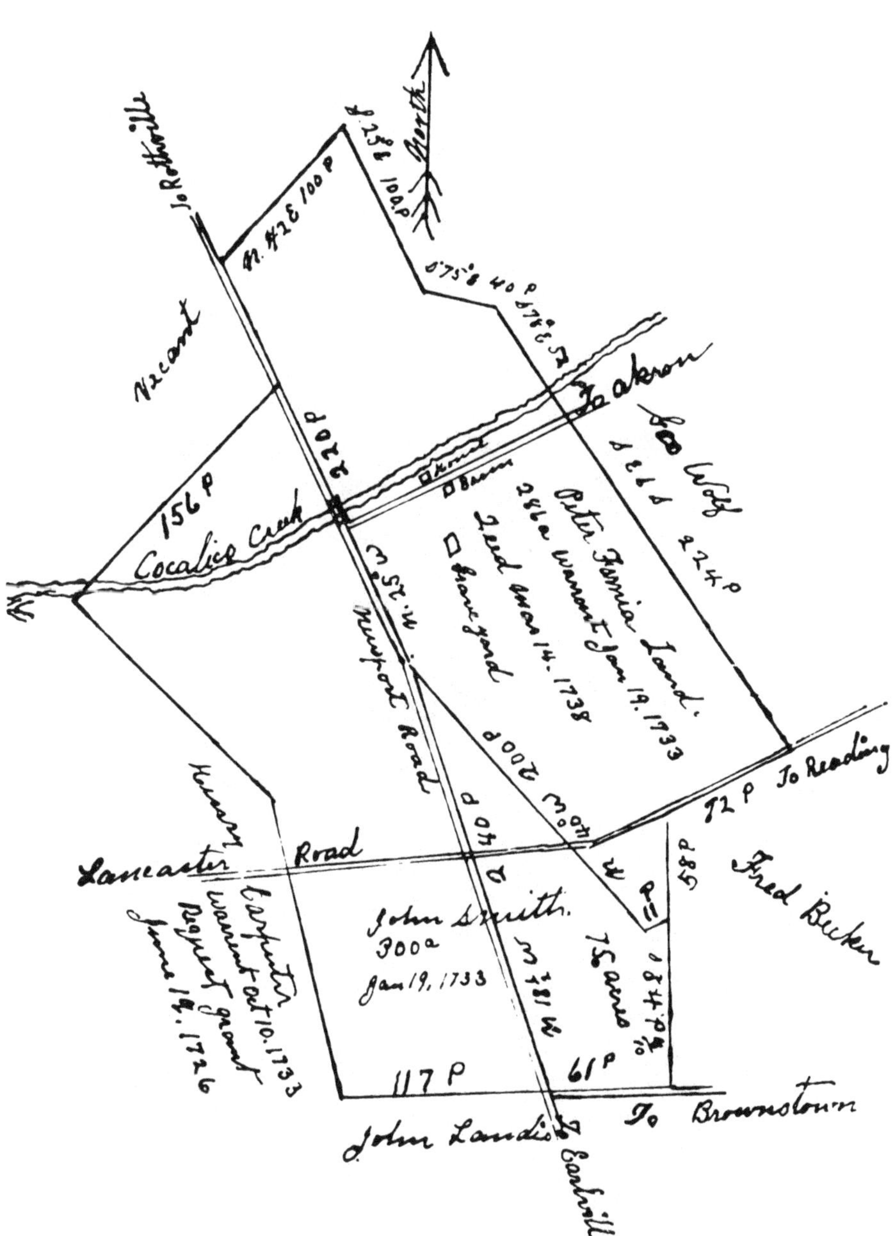

Boundaries of Forney and Smith Farms, Original Grant

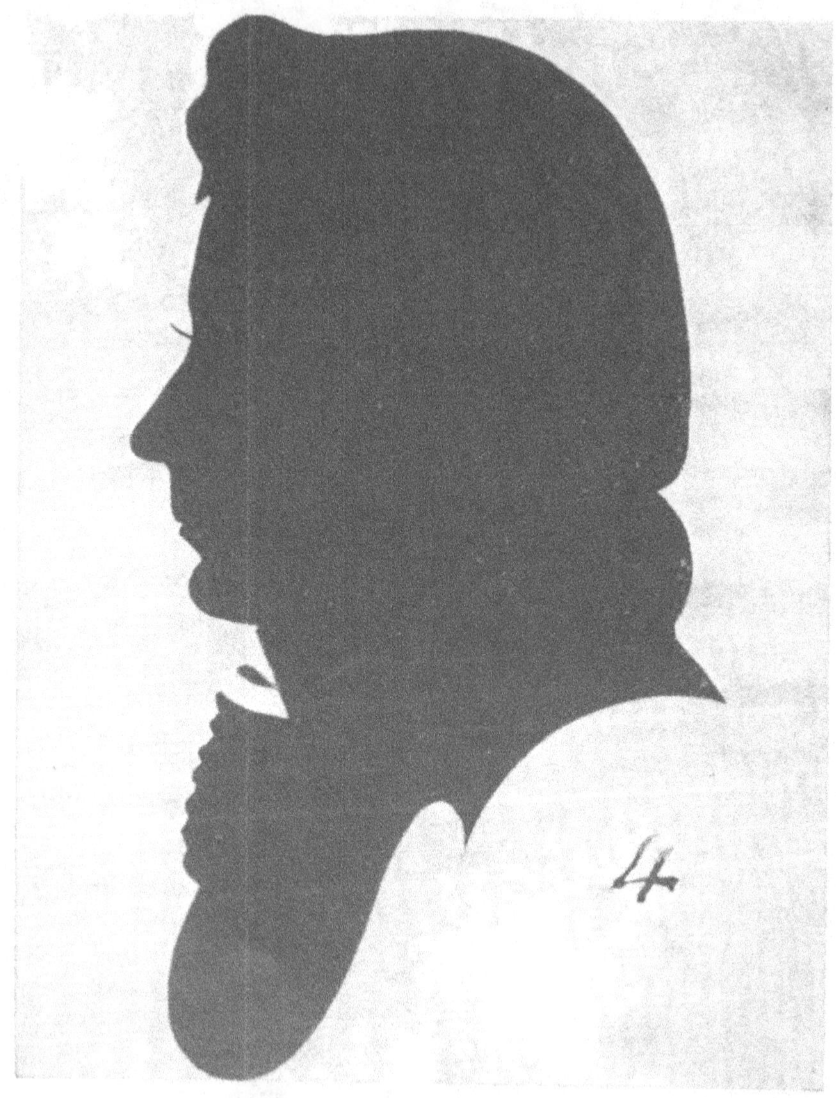

JOHN WEIDMAN FORNEY
Taken 1805

J. K. FORNEY
Taken 1917

A. FORNEY SERVED IN THE REVOLUTIONARY WAR

April 28, 1914.

TO WHOM IT MAY CONCERN:-

I hereby Certify that one ABRAHAM FORNEY was a Private in Captain John Lutz's Company, Fifth Battalion, Lancaster County Militia, 1781.

See p. 482, Volume Seven, Pennsylvania Archives, Fifth Series.

Luther R. Kelker

Custodian of the Public Records.

In testimony whereof
I hereby affix the Seal
of this Department

SON OF A. FORNEY SERVED IN THE REVOLUTIONARY ARMY

April 28, 1914.

TO WHOM IT MAY CONCERN:-

I hereby Certify that one ABRHAM FORNY, JUNR., was a Private in Captain Stattler's Company, Lancaster County Militia, 1781.

See p. 477, Volume Seven, Pennsylvania Archives, Fifth Series.

Luther R. Kelker
Custodian of the Public Records.

In testimony whereof
I hereby affix the Seal
of this Department

SON OF A. FORNEY
SERVED IN THE REVOLUTIONARY ARMY

April 28, 1914.

TO WHOM IT MAY CONCERN:-

I hereby Certify that one JOHN FORNEY was a Private in Captain Patrick Hays' Company, Ninth Battalion, Lancaster County Militia, 1781.

Colonel, John Rogers.

See p. 932, Volume Seven, Pennsylvania Archives, Fifth Series.

Luther R. Kelker
Custodian of the Public Records.

In testimony whereof
I hereby affix the Seal
of this Department

SON OF A. FORNEY SERVED IN THE REVOLUTIONARY ARMY

April 10, 1916.

TO WHOM IT MAY CONCERN:-

I hereby Certify that one PETER FORNEY was a Private in Captain Patrick Hays' Company, Ninth Battalion, Lancaster County Militia, commanded by Colonel John Rogers, 1781.

See p. 932, Volume Seven, Pennsylvania Archives, Fifth Series.

State Librarian.

In testimony whereof
I hereby Affix the Seal
of this Department

NEPHEW OF A. FORNEY, SERVED IN THE REVOLUTIONARY ARMY

TO WHOM IT MAY CONCERN:-

I hereby certify to the Revolutionary services of Peter Forney as follows:-

Peter Forney was a private in Capt. John Lesher's Company, Lt.Col. John Patton, of Berks county, battalion of foot, of Penna. Militia August 27, 1776. For reference see page ~~248~~ 56, Vol.14, Second Series, Penna. Archives.

Very truly yours,

Geo Edward Reed

State Librarian and Editor Penna. Archives.

COMMONWEALTH OF PENNSYLVANIA LIBRARY DEPARTMENT

THE OLD GRAVEYARD FENCE
Was 43½x43½ Feet Square

TAKEN FROM THE WILL OF A. ELIZABETH FORNEY, MADE SEPTEMBER 28, 1907, AND RECORDED IN DEED BOOK "U"—PAGE 484, ITEM 1

I give and bequeath to the Zion Lutheran Church of Mechanicsburg, in Upper Leacock Township, Lancaster County, Pa., the sum of $400.00, the interest thereof to be used to keep the Forney graveyard in West Earl Township, Lancaster County, Pa., clean and in good repairs, to be cleaned twice a year, half of the interest to be used to replace the fence if needed, and the other half to the sexton to keep the graveyard clean.

If this Graveyard will be provided for to be kept in good order before my decease, then this bequest shall go to the Zion Lutheran Church of Mechanicsburg in Upper Leacock Township, Lancaster County, Pa., the income to be used for Pastor's salary of said church.

A. Elizabeth Forney died April 5, 1912.

MONUMENT WHEN VEILED

MONUMENT UNVEILED

MONUMENTS ENCLOSED BY WALL

MONUMENT UNVEILED

Unveil Tablet to Ancestors of Forney Family

One hundred and three members of the Forney family held a reunion on Friday morning, May 30, 1919, near Brownstown, and unveiled a monument to the illustrious dead of the family burial ground there. Five of the forebears of the old house fought with Washington's army in the Revolutionary War. There were two Peters, Abe senior and junior, and John Forney. The monument which is 6 feet high and of Vermont granite was unveiled with due ceremony and an interesting program had been prepared which included the formation of a permanent association by the Forney family.

The following is a list of the Forney's that attended the unveiling of the monument:

John K. Forney, Abilene, Kansas; Rev. M. G. Forney and wife, Paul Forney, East Petersburg; Rev. Roy Forney, East Petersburg; Miss Ruth Forney, Mr. and Mrs. Albert Groff, East Petersburg; Mr. and Mrs. J. G. Forney, Lancaster; Mary Elizabeth and Helen Frances Forney, Lancaster; Mr. and Mrs. A. L. Hostetter, Ruth F. Hostetter, Paul F. Hostetter, Manheim, R. 1; T. N. Hostetter, Jay Forney Hostetter, Pottsville, Pa.; Geo. A. Hostetter, Nettie Hostetter, Emma Hostetter, Lancaster; Mr. and Mrs. S. P. Gingrich, East Petersburg; Martin K. Forney, Mr. and Mrs. J. H. Eshleman, Ruth Eshleman, Elizabethtown; Mr. and Mrs. Lane Forney, Esther Forney, Nettie Forney, Galen Forney, Lititz; Mrs. Maria Graybill, Lititz; Mr. and Mrs. Earl Rohrer, Lititz; Clayton Sheaffer, Mary Sheaffer, Bareville; Mr. and Mrs. John H. Hertzler, Mt. Joy; Mr. and Mrs. John F. Nissley, Virginia Nissley, Hiram G. Mentzer, Edna Forney Mentzer, Ephrata; Maribell Nissley, Lancaster, Pa.; Miss Mary Lane Johns, Lancaster, Pa.; Mr. and Mrs. Mahlon Garman, Martin R. Forney, Dorothy Garman, Martha Garman, Wilbur Garman, Lititz, Pa.; Ezra Zucher, Mrs. Lizzie Zercher, Beulah Zercher, Martha Zercher, John K. Young, Mr. and Mrs. Roy H. Young, Mt. Joy; Mr. and Mrs. Roy H. Young, Mt. Joy; Mr. and Mrs. Oscar H. Rube, Chester Y. Rule, Vera Y. Rule, Manheim, R. 4.; Mr. and Mrs. J. H. Young, Mt. Joy; Mr. and Mrs. Oscar H. Rule, Chester Y. John F. Longenecker, John F. Longenecker, Jr., Lititz; Mr. and Mrs. John Wissler, Lititz; Mr. and Mrs. William Strickler, Lebanon; Mr. and Mrs. Stanton V. von Graybill, Master Stanton S. von Graybill, Lancaster, Pa.; Mr. and Mrs. Cyrus Strickler, Lebanon; Dr. and Mrs. H. W. George, Dorothy Forney, George Forney, Helen Forney George, Mary Forney George, Middletown; Mr. and Mrs. A. F. Longenecker, Akron; Abram H. Forney, Elizabethtown; Mr. and Mrs. A. G. Strickler, Lee Forney Strickler, Roy G. Strickler, Edward K. Strickler, Patterson, N. J.

Program: Unveiling of monument by Mary Elizabeth Forney and singing "My Country 'Tis of Thee." Invocation, Rev. M. G. Forney; historical address by John K. Forney of Abilene, Kansas; patriotic address by J. G. Forney; forming a permanent organization; President, John K. Forney, Abilene, Kansas; 1st vice president, J. G. Forney, Lancaster, Pa,; 2nd vice president, Rev. M. G. Forney, East Petersburg; secretary, Mrs. Elizabeth Forney Gingrich; treasurer, Mary Lane Johns, Lancaster, Pa.

LANDING OF THE FORNEYS IN THE NEW WORLD

Forney landings at Philadelphia, Penna, Pennsylvania Archives. Second Series, Vol. 17, Page 8, landed Sept. 18, 1827. Ship William Sarah. William Hill Master. Abraham Farne and his only brother, John Farne, age 15 years, they at once made their way inland to the Lancaster County colony. Qualified to be true and faithful to King George and the province of Pennsylvania. Vol. 3, Page 283. Colonial records. This boy John is the father of Dr. Peter Fahrney, Beaver Creek, Maryland.—Dr. Peter Fahrney House Journal, Chicago, Ill.

Vol. 17, Pages 110, 112, Sept. 23, 1734. Ship Hope Daniel Reed Master. Christian Farnia, age 27, Ann Eliza. Farnia, age 23; Catharine Farnia, age 29. Settled in Earl and Warwick townships, Lancaster County, Penna.

Vol. 17, Pages 131-132, Aug. 30, 1737. Ship Samuel Hugh Percy Master, Abraham Farni or Abraham Funfurney age 64. No record of settlement. Luther R. Kelger late custodian of the public records, Harrisburg, Penna, claimed. Old Abraham, was the father of all the Forneys of Lancaster, Lebanon and Dauphin counties, Penna.

Vol. 17, Pages 190, 192, Sept. 3, 1739. Ship Friendship. William Vittery commander. Jacob Farne age 18 years.

Page 357, Sept. 23, 1752. Ship St. Andrews, Capt. James Abercrombia master. Jacob Forne, sick. Second time to America. Settled in Lincoln County, North Carolina in 1754.

Vol. 17, Page 291, Sept. 15, 1749. Ship Phoenix, John Mason, Master John Farni. No record of settlement.

Vol. 17, Page 325, Nov. 3, 1750. Ship Brotherhood, John Thompson, Captain. Joseph Fahrene and Peter Fahrene, Lebanon and Dauphin County, Pa.—H. O. F.

Vol. 17, Page 338, Sept. 16, 1751. Ship Brothers, William Muir, Captain. Hans Jacob Marni. No record of settlement.

Vol. 17, Page 489, Oct. 13, 1769. Ship Minerva, Thomas Arnott, Captain. Joseph Farni and Jacob Farni, Cumberland County, Penna.—H. O. F.

John Adam Forney arrived at Philadelphia Oct. 16, 1721. He remained in Philadelphia County for some years and in 1734 moved his family to Diggss Choice, what is now Hanover, York County, Penna., and remained and died in 1752.—Lucy Forney Bittinger.

Peter Forney and wife Ann Smith landed at Philadelphia before 1727. Located in Earl Township, Lancaster County, Penna., and he died July 1747.

John Forney, Cocalico Township (Reamstown), Lancaster County, Penna., he also settled there before 1727. A brief school history of Lancaster County by Israel Smith Clare. Notes settlement of Reamstown, Lancaster County, by Everhard Ream, in 1723. Mentions the name Forney as a neighbor soon after he located there, and there was also a younger brother Joseph, and a sister, Magdaline, specially mentioned, came from the Old Country. She married Daniel Carpenter, fourth son of Dr. Henry Carpenter and Salome Ruffner. John died 1769.

WILL OF JOHN FORNEY OF REAMSTOWN

Book A, Vol. 1, Page 244. John Forney, deceased. The last will and testament of John Forney, deceased, written in High Dutch, could not be recorded but thereon is endorsed as follows:

Book X, Vol. 2, Page 147.

John Fahrne, deceased.

In the Name of God Amen. I John Fahrny, am very sick on my body yet of good and Sound Understanding thanks be to God to this very day viz the twentieth of March 1769. I acknowledge and did use in this very last will and Testament and it shall be as followeth viz First shall Joseph Fahrny and Michael Bare Junior be my executors.

Secondly. All my Estate shall be valued and sold and from this shall be paid all which have a demand against me. Further the rest due of my estate shall be divided amongst my four children in equal shares viz to my daughter Barbara Fahrny to my son Jacob Fahrny to my Daughter Catharine Fahrny and to my son Peter Farhny. I John Fahrny living in Co. Collico Township in Lancaster County testify this to be my last Will and Testament with my own hand and seal the day and year aforesaid. John Fahrney. Witnesses John Zug Andrew Ream.

John Fahrne is the correct signature.

Book A Vol. 1, Page 244.

Be it Remembered that on the Seventeenth Day of April, Anno Domine 1769. The last Will and Testament of John Forney, late of County of Lancaster, Yoeman deceased, was proved in due form of Law and Letters Testamentary thereon were granted to Joseph Forney and Michael Bare the Executors therein named they be first duly Qualified Well and Truly to Administer the Estate of the said decedent and to Exhibit a true and perfect Inventory thereof into the Registers Office at Lancaster on or before the Seventeenth Day of May next, and to render a true and just account of their administration. When there to Lawfully required Given under the Seal of the said office and me.

Edw. Shippen, D. R.

HISTORY AND PART GENEALOGY OF JOHN FORNEY

There are no later records from any of this Forney's family at the court house at Lancaster, and indications are that Joseph and his nephew, Peter emigrated to Sommerset county with the Rev. Peter Livengood who went from Berks County, Pa., to Sommerset County, Pa., in about 1772 and we find that Joseph Fahrne had surveyed to him Dec. 15, 1774 some land in Bedford County, Pa., in Brothers Valley Township on tract known as Maple Swamp. It now locates in Summet Twp. Sommerset Co., Pa. In 1783 he had 200 acres and Peter Fahrene, his nephew, had 100 acres. It is presumed they are the same Forneys that lived at Reamstown, and the proof is, that the Forneys from Sommerset County came frequently to the home of the writer's great grandfather and grand father and even to the time of my father's boyhood days in his father's home, and stayed over night with them when they came through to visit some of their relatives at Reamstown, and Berks County, Pa., and will now give a genealogy line of a few of them.

1......John Fahrne, Reamstown, Pa., d. April 1769.
2......Magdalena Farhne, Reamstown, Pa. M. Daniel Carpenter, Earlville, Pa., b. 1717, fourth son of Dr. Henry Carpenter and Salome Ruffner.
3......Joseph Fahrne, Sommerset Co., Pa.

Family of JOHN FAHRNE (1)

4......Barbara, Reamstown, Pa. M. Michael Bare.
5......Jacob, Reamstown, Pa.
6......Catharine, Reamstown, Pa.
7......Peter, Berlin, Sommerset Co., Pa.

Family of JOSEPH FAHRNE (3)

8......Elizabeth, Sommerset Co., Pa. B. 1769; d. 1849. M. Christian Livengood, b. 1761; d. 1837.

Family of PETER FAHRNY (7)

9......Abraham, Harrison Co., Ohio and Westward.

10......Christian, Harrison Co., Ohio and Westward.

11......John, Berlin, Pa. B. Nov. 1777; d. Sept. 20, 1846. M. Susan Beaghley.

12......Peter, Mound City, Mo., b. 1780; d. 1871.

Family of JOHN FORNEY (11) and SUSAN BEAGHLEY

13......Elizabeth. M. Strausser.

14......Jacob.

15......Samuel.

16......Michael, b. 1811; d. 1895.

17......Catharine, b. 1813. M. Horner.

18......John, Abilene, Kansas, b. April 25, 1815; d. Feb. 6, 1896. M. Eva Horner and Eles Ann Stahl.

19......Sarah. M. Miller.

20......Joseph.

21......Daniel.

22......Eli.

23......Peter, Glendale, Ariz., b. Nov. 28, 1828; d. Dec. 25, 1915. M. Polly Cover.

LETTER FROM REV. PETER FORNEY

J. K. Forney,
Abilene, Kansas.

Dear Sir: Your letter of inquiry came to hand today; contents perused. In answer will say I know but very little about my ancestors. I was the youngest of my father's family and never heard very much of our ancestry. My father had three brothers, Abraham, Christian and Peter. They all went west to Ohio in early days. I don't know that they ever came back. When my father died in 1846 they did not know where to write to inform any of them. But after my brother John moved to Nebraska or Kansas, he came across Uncle Peter who was the youngest of my uncles, and was then ninety years old. My father John was an elder in our church and traveled considerably in his time and was then the only Forney family in Sommerset County, Pa. I was 17 years old when my father died. What part of Germany my ancestors came from, I am not able to tell but think they lived in eastern Pennsylvania. Sometime as they said we have some relatives there. My father spelled his name in German Fahrney and in English Forney, so of course the children all were Forneys and not Fahrney.

Yours in love,
PETER FORNEY.

A WONDERFUL FAMILY RECORD

Elder John Forney of Buckeye township, this county, made the Gazette a friendly and welcome visit last Saturday. At our request he gave us a brief record of his family, in compliance with the desire of his children who wish to preserve this issue of the Gazette in their families. The venerable patriarch handed us the following list, dated August 31, 1894, which is as far as he knows correct to that date:

By my first wife, Eve (Horner), were born to me five sons, and by my second wife Eles Ann (Stahl), were born seven sons and seven daughters—19 children, as follows:

Children	Grand Children		Great Grand Children	
William Forney *	5	1*	5	1*
Christian Forney	8		5	
Samuel Forney	10	2*	5	1*
Jacob Forney*	4	2*	2	
Michael Forney*	11	4*	5	
Susannah Judy	6	2*	2	
Sally Royer	3			
Harrietta Stump	13	2*		
Jeremiah Forney	12	4*	1	
Catharine Shick	7			
Mary Neely	3			
John J. Forney	2			
Benjamin Forney	7	3*		
Abraham Forney				
Peter Forney				
Isaac Forney	7	1*		
Amanda Arnold				
Eles-Ann Miller	4			
Elijah Forney	1			
Total Children 19	103	21	25	2
Grand Total 147				

*Deceased.

By the above you can all see that the number of souls still alive as far as known are:

My own children	16
Grandchildren	82
Great grandchildren	23
Total	121

Out of the 147 there have been 26 deaths up to the present.
I am in my 80th year since April 25, 1894.

JOHN FORNEY, Sr.

The above is an unusual and wonderful family record—a record of a family whose members we believe will average well as good and useful citizens and are doing their full share, towards making the world better and happier.

Elder John Forney was born in Somerset county, Pa. He is a member of the Brethren (German Baptist Church), sometimes called "Dunkard," and has preached the Gospel during a period of more than fifty-five years—and though in his 80th year is still a strong and able preacher and an honest man, one of the noblest workers of God. May the useful life of the venerable preacher be prolonged yet many years.—Abilene Gazette.

FAMILY RECORD OF ELDER JOHN FORNEY, JANUARY, 1926

Children	Grand Children		Great Grand Children		G. G. Grand Children		G. G. G. Children
	B.	D.	B.	D.	B.	D.	Born
William Forney*	5	3	4				
Christian Forney*	8	3	11	1	6		
Samuel Forney*	11	2	22	3	10	1	2
Jacob Forney*	4	2	5	2	8		
Michael Forney*	11	5	25	6	17	3	
Susanah Judy	6	3	5		2		
Sally Royer	3		2				
Harrietta Stump	13	5	31	2	16	2	
Jeremiah Forney	12	6	12		7		
Catharine Shick	7		8				
Mary Neely	3	1	7		3		
John J. Forney	3		4				
Benjamin Forney*	8	4	2				
Abraham Forney*	1		2				
Peter Forney							
Isaac Forney	7	1	7				
Amanda Arnold*							
Eles-Ann Miller	8	2	5				
Elijah Forney	3		1				
Total 19	113	37	153	14	69	6	2

*Deceased 9.
Total Decendants 356. Now living 290.

RECORD OF FORNEYS IN REVOLUTIONARY WAR

Abraham Forney, Sr., was a private in Capt. Emanuel Carpenter's Seventh Co., Tenth Bat., Lancaster County Militia; Col. David Jenkins. See p. 987, Vol. 7, Pennsylvania archives. Fifth Series. 1777.

Abraham Forney, Jr., was a private in Capt. Emanuel Carpenter's Seventh Co., Tenth Bat., Lancaster County Militia. Col. David Jenkins. See p. 987, Vol. 7, Pennsylvania archives. Fifth Series. 1777.

Abraham Forney, Sr., was a private in Capt. John Lutz's Co., Fifth Bat., Lancaster County Militia. Tour of duty Sept. 22, 1781—Oct. 11, 1781. See p. 482, Vol. 7, Pennsylvania archives. Fifth Series.

Abraham Forney, Jr., was a private in Capt. Rudy Strattler's Co., Lancaster County Militia. Mustered out June 2, 1781. See p. 477, Vol. 7, Pennsylvania archives. Fifth Series.

John Forney was a private in Capt. Patrick Hays' Co., Ninth Bat., Lancaster County Militia. Col. John Rogers. See p. 932-951, Vol. 7, Pennsylvania archives. Fifth Series, Nov. 17, 1781.

Peter Forney was a private in Capt. Patrick Hays' Co., Ninth Bat., Lancaster County Militia. Col. John Rogers. See p. 932, Vol. 7, Pennsylvania archives. Fifth Series, 1781.

Peter Forney was a private in Capt. John Lesher's Co. Lt. Col. John Patton Bat., Berks County Militia. See p. 256, Vol. 14, Pennsylvania, Second Series, Aug. 27, 1776.

Christ Forney was a private in Capt. Emanuel Carpenter's 7th Co., Tenth Bat., Lancaster County Militia. Col. David Jenkins. See p. 987, Vol. 7, Pennsylvania archives. Fifth Series 1777.

Christ Forney was a private in Capt. Patrick Hays' Second Co., Ninth Bat., Lancaster County Militia. Col. John Rogers. See p. 867-931, Vol. 7, Pennsylvania archives. Fifth Series, Nov. 17 1781.

John Forney was a private in Capt. Patrick Hays' Second Co., Eighth Bat., May 24, 1779. Absent five days and in Fifth Co., Sixth Bat. Aug. 18, 1779. Lancaster County Militia. Col. John Rogers. See p. 553, 562, 868, Vol. 7, Pennsylvania archives. Fifth Series.

John Forney was a private in Capt. Kempline Northumberland County Militia. Enlisted May 7, 1779. Firty-five years, height 5 ft., 3-in.; complexion dark; trade barber; born in Canada. See p. 365, 775, Vol. 4, Pennsylvania archives. Fifth Series.

Anthony Forney, p. 1098, Vol. 2, Fifth Series, Pennsylvania archives.

Christoly Forney, p. 73, Vol. 7. Fifth Series. Pennsylvania archives.

John Forney, p. 73, Vol. 7. Fifth Series. Pennsylvania archives.

Joseph Forney, p. 867, Vol. 7. Fifth Series. Pennsylvania archives.

Peter Forney, pp. 73, 868, 932, Vol. 7. Fifth Series. Pennsylvania archives.

Robert Forney, p. 987 Vol. 7. Fifth Series. Pennsylvania archives.

www.ingramcontent.com/pod-product-compliance
Lightning Source LLC
Chambersburg PA
CBHW060346100426
42812CB00003B/1148

* 9 7 8 1 5 9 6 4 1 3 0 8 5 *